Quality Management

Communication and Project Management

Mary-Clare Bushell PhD MBA

Quality Management & Training (Publications) Limited
PO Box 172 Guildford Surrey United Kingdom GU2 7FN
Telephone: +44 (0) 1256 358083 or +44 (0) 1483 453511 **Fax:** +44 (0) 1483 453512
E-mail: help@qmt.co.uk **Website**: www.qmt.co.uk

Quality Management & Training (Publications) Limited
PO Box 172 Guildford Surrey GU2 7FN

First Published by Quality Management & Training (Publications) Limited
2002

All rights reserved. No part of this publication may be reproduced in any material form including photocopying, or storing in any medium by electronic means and whether or not transiently or incidentally to some other use of this publication without the written permission of the Copyright holder except in accordance with the provision of the Copyright, Designs and Patents Act 1988 or under the terms of a licence issued by the Copyright Licensing Agency Limited, 90 Tottenham Court Road, London, W1P 9HE, England. Applications for copyright holder's permission to reproduce any part of this publication should be addressed to the publishers.

British Library Cataloguing in publications data

A catalogue record for this book is available from the British Library

ISBN   1-904302-06-8

Printed and Bound in Great Britain by:
Biddles Limited
Woodbridge Park Estate, Woodbridge Road, Guildford, Surrey GU1 1DA

Table of Contents

Table of Contents 3
Introduction to Communication and Project Management 5
Theories, Models and Essential Terms 9
    The Communication Process... 10
Barriers to Communication 14
Messages, Media and Channels... 16
    Oral Communication.. 17
    Written Communication.. 22
    Non-Verbal Communication 25
Using language and using images 26
    The uses of language 26
    Techniques for Good Business Writing 27
    Layout and Formats... 34
    Using Illustrations and Images 39
Powers of Persuasion, Motivation and Change........................... 43
Information Gathering and Research Activities........................... 49
    Information Gathering.. 49
    Literature Surveys 54
    Recording and sorting your findings 56

Analysis and Presentation of Data... 60

Qualitative and Quantitative Data 60
Report Writing.. 65
Making Presentations 72
    Preparation for Communicating 72
    Planning the Message 73
    Preparation 74
    Giving your talk 75
Group Communication 77
    Advantages of Groups 77
    Disadvantages of Groups 80
    Group Effectiveness 80
    Group Interaction 82
Project Definition 89
The Project Environment 92
Projects and Company Organisation Structure 95
    Functional Organisation 96

- Project based Organisation 98
- Matrix Organisation 99
- Project Life Cycle 102
  - Phases in the Project Life Cycle 104
- Work breakdown structures (WBS) 110
- Control and Review of Projects 114
  - Project Documentation 114
  - Change Control 116
  - Reactive Control 118
  - Proactive Control and Project Review 120
  - Corrective and Preventive Action 127
  - Project Final Report 127
  - Project Audits 129
- Planning Concepts 133
- Managing the planning process 136
  - Goals, Constraints and Requirements 136
  - Work Breakdown Structure and Networking 139
  - Scheduling and Timescales 139
  - Budget 139
  - The Final Plan 145
- Networking 145
  - Activity on Node (AoN) 147
  - Activity on Arrow (AoA) 150
- PERT and Critical Path Analysis 152
  - Time Schedule 153
- Why have Quality Assurance in Projects? 163
- Project Quality Management Processes 165
- Quality Planning 166
  - Quality Plan 166
- Quality Control 174
- Quality Assurance 175
- Quality Management Tools 177
- BS ISO 10006: 1997 184
  - Guidelines to Quality in Project Management 184
- BS 6079:2000 185

Introduction to Communication and Project Management

This book has been developed to support the Institute of Quality Assurance diploma course D4. The first half is intended to enhance the students' ability to become more effective communicators by developing the transferable skills of communication and presentation. The second half introduces the student to the techniques and applications of project management.

The book is in five sections:

Section One:

This section is intended to provide sufficient information to:
- Demonstrate an understanding of the key concepts of communication theory
- Identify and apply the principles of effective communication to enhance communication practice internal and external to the organisation

Section Two

This section is intended to provide sufficient information to:
- Select and evaluate research methods
- Present information effectively in both written and oral format
- Understand group dynamics and the ability to interact and lead a group effectively

Section Three

This section is intended to provide sufficient information to:
- Understand the nature and context of project management in specific circumstances
- Understand the Project Life Cycle
- Understand the application of Work Breakdown Structure
- Understand the functions of project control and review

Section Four

This section is intended to provide sufficient information to:
- Apply and appraise appropriate project networking techniques
- Apply and appraise appropriate project management and project planning techniques in given circumstances

Section Five

This section is intended to provide sufficient information to:
- Understand the importance of quality in project management
- Use quality standards to assist in ensuring that quality is reflected in the project process

The book was written in a way that hopefully makes the various techniques and approaches to Communication and Project Management self-explanatory. However, if the reader has any problems with the contents or has a quality problem or issue that they would like to discuss further, please do not hesitate to contact me. I can be contacted via the publishers - I welcome the opportunity to discuss quality issues. help@qmt.co.uk

The book has been written by Mary-Clare Bushell with contributions from Geoff Vorley, Edda Saunders and Jill Crow.

Thanks to Brian, Richard and Michael for being so patience during the writing of this book.

Section 1

Communication

Communication

Theories, Models and Essential Terms

I know you believe that you understand what you think I said, but I am not sure whether you realise that what you heard is not what I meant. [Anon]

Have you ever felt like that? Have you ever said – or heard someone say – "I didn't really mean that", or "You haven't grasped my point"?

Communicating is something we've been doing since birth; a baby's first cry is its first reaction to the world, and a mother quickly learns whether the baby's cry signals hunger, tiredness or discomfort. Communication is human interaction; 90% of our lives is spent communicating.

Why then, as we grow up, does it become so fraught with difficulties and problems? How is it that sometimes things get in the way and we are not understood in the way that we intended? Why, even when we are understood, do we often fail to get people to think or behave in the way we want them to?

And a final question .... if it is all so difficult, how do we ever manage to get our message across?

It's not what we say; it's the way that we say it.

It's a fact of life that we all see ourselves as being able to communicate pretty well – we've been doing it for long enough. But think of all the phrases we have for describing the way that people communicate:

- ..... always speaks her mind
- ..... doesn't believe in beating about the bush
- ..... speaks before he thinks
- ..... calls a spade a spade
- ..... opens her mouth and puts her foot right in it
- ..... says the wrong thing
- ..... not what he says but the way that he says it.

Some of these phrases refer to getting it right, but the majority imply that the person being described is somehow getting it wrong. All too often there is a mismatch, intentional or not, between what we say and what others understand us to mean.

Communication

When this happens at work, consequences can sometimes be far-reaching and disastrous. At the very least they can give rise to frustration, offence, instructions that are difficult to follow, or poor customer relations.

So what's the answer?

It is always possible to get good results by chance. After all, we have been improving our skills since infancy, to a greater or lesser degree of success. But what distinguishes skilled communicators from average ones is that they consistently get the desired results with the minimum of effort in the minimum time.

Just as manual skills can be learnt and practiced, so can communication skills. In this section you will not so much be learning new skills as developing and perfecting skills you already possess. You will be smoothing your path through the communications maze and contributing to the effective communications that are vital to the efficient operation of any organisation.

- Communication is a two-way process
- Communication happens on several levels
- What we feel affects the way we communicate
- Communication is about understanding as well as talking (or writing)

And lastly:
- Effective communication should start with realistic self-awareness!

The Communication Process

Let's start by analysing what happens when two people – say you and I – hold a conversation:

1 I think of something I want to say to you. I then have to start by gaining your attention; having done this, I now speak to convey my message.
2 You listen to and – hopefully – take in what I have said.

Communication

3   As the listener, you will feel something about the message, and will also interpret it in the context of your own perceptions. This is where misinterpretations may arise – your feelings and attitudes may get in the way - your understanding of the way words are used might be different from mine. Whatever the reason, you then respond in a particular way – which may or may not be what I expected.

Put simply, the process of communicating involves a number of steps during which a message is conceived, put into words, and sent to a receiver who then interprets it and responds.

This can best be understood by analysing it into a cyclical flow diagram:

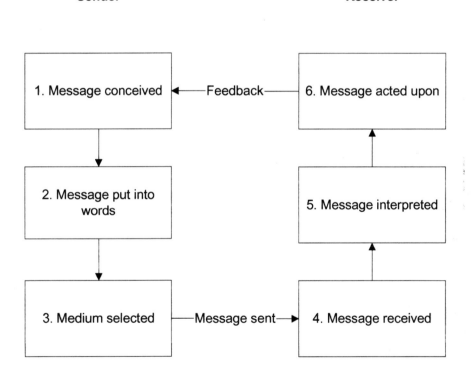

Figure 1.1 The Communication Process

Communication

This may seem complex, but in fact it is quite logical. Let us go on to analyse the steps in detail.

Step 1: Message conceived

The decision to send a message may be quite involuntary, or it may be the result of careful reasoning. Whichever it is, all communication has an objective, or purpose – something we want to happen as a result. Whatever we want to communicate and achieve, we will have four *general* objectives:

- to be received (heard or read)
- to be understood
- to be accepted
- to get a response

If we fail in any of these then we have failed to communicate. This can lead to resentment and frustration and is often expressed as "Can't you understand plain English?"

Step 2: Message put into words

The choice of appropriate 'language' plays a large part in the ultimate success of the message. The languages of communication include:

- spoken words
- written words
- numbers
- symbols, pictures or diagrams
- body language

Step 3: Medium selected

The medium is the 'vehicle' by which the message is sent. The choice of medium is again crucial to the success of the message. Some messages need to be written, others spoken. A formal report may be chosen as the best vehicle for organising and studying complex information. A disciplinary message is better given in a formal interview rather than in a busy open-plan office. A large amount of data may be expressed more clearly in a chart rather than by spoken or written words.

Communication

Step 4: Message received

Often a message fails to be received because the sender uses the wrong language. 'Jargon' or 'officialese' are frequently the culprits, but it could simply be that the receiver, for example, cannot read a graph. There are many potential barriers to the successful receipt of a message; these can include:

- language – wrong words, dialect words, jargon, 'waffle' etc
- psychological – personality clashes, attitudes, feelings, pre-judging a situation
- physical – poor timing, interruptions, distractions……

(The barriers to communication will be considered in more detail later on in this section.)

Step 5: Message interpreted

As well as understanding the language, the receiver has to be able to interpret the message correctly. Many messages are made up of the apparent meaning and the underlying one; and the context of a message can affect the way in which it is interpreted.

Step 6: Message acted upon

Action as a result of an interpreted message may simply be a smile, a nod, a yawn or a silence. It may be the answer to a question, or actions carried out as the result of instructions. Whichever it is, this step provides feedback to the sender letting them know that the message has been:

- received
- understood
- interpreted correctly (or incorrectly)

Feedback is essential to effective communication as it informs the sender that the message is successful, or that a different choice of language or medium is called for. The sender must always be able to recognise and interpret feedback signals.

Communication

Listening

An essential part of the oral communication process is actually listening. Often people are so busy concentrating on the next point they want to make, that they do not listen to what the other person is saying.

In an average day about two thirds of the time is spent listening. There are valid reasons for improving your listening skills.

- Encouraging others. When people see you are interested they are more likely to relax and their communication will improve.
- Gaining information. Effective listening will help you obtain as much relevant information as possible.
- Resolving problems. Problems can best be solved when people listen to each other and try to understand the other person's point of view.

How can you improve your listening skills? Concentrate on the speaker, listen to the ideas and concepts that are being presented, try and summarise what they are saying, does it make sense, is it accurate and objective, is the argument strong? Do not assume that it will be boring – cut out the irrelevant stuff and try to find relevant information.

Barriers to Communication

Communication is not always successful; there are many types of barrier that can prevent communication.

- *Uncertainty of Message* - We are not sure what to say. This could be because we are not sure how much the receiver needs to know, how it will affect them, or whether we should use some examples to illustrate it. It can be eased in face-to-face communication because we can respond to the receiver and see where extra information is needed or where information has not been understood. In written communication we no longer have that immediate feedback available, although we do have time to plan the communication more carefully. If you are worried about your written communication, then ask a colleague to read it and if possible put it aside for a day or two and then re-read it and revise it with fresh eyes.

Communication

- *Faulty Presentation* - The message may be presented poorly. The message maybe badly expressed or maybe confusing. Alternatively, using an incorrect medium may upset the receiver such that the message is not clearly received. Finally, the chosen medium could have been used badly e.g. the overhead slide had too much information on it.
- *Limited Capacity of Target* - The receiver may not be able to understand the message. If a scientific theory is to be presented to a general audience, the speaker must adjust his presentation or he will not be understood. In general, figures and calculations tend to switch people off and this type of information is often easier to understand in graphical or picture format.
- *Unstated Assumptions* - If the sender and receiver have different assumptions about some aspect of the message and are unaware that they are different, then the communication may fail. The Charge of the Light Brigade is a well-known example. The British troops attacked the 'enemy' as they had been ordered to do. However, the sender was only referring to a small detachment of the enemy, not the massed ranks that were visible to the attacking troops. The lack of communication arises not because we have failed to understand a message but because, unknown to us, we have misunderstood it.
- *Incompatible Viewpoints* - Communication between people may fail because they see the world from a different point of view. For example: Arabs and Israelis may not be able to resolve their differences by talking, because almost anything the other side says will be disputed. This is why intermediaries are so important; they try and interpret the issues for each side.
- *Deception* - A person decides not to tell other people, or the communication is ambiguous. Communicating 'disinformation' is more common than you might think. How often are you 'economical with the truth'? Disinformation has also been used to great effect in wars.
- *Interference and Distraction* - If the communication process is disrupted then this can interfere with the understanding. This could be a telephone call during a face-to-face conversation, or your receiver on the other end of the phone may be trying to finish something else whilst only half listening to you. In a presentation the interference could be environmental – a hot stuffy room will certainly interfere with the concentration of the receivers in the room.
- *Lack of Channels* - There may not be a suitable channel for the communication.

Communication

- *Too many in the Chain* - The 'Chinese whispers' problem. If a message has had to go through many other people then there is a high chance that the message will become corrupted.
- *Physical* - Poor timing – e.g. you telephoned at the wrong time and the receiver is not really ready to listen.
- *Language* - Using poorly understood words; these could be technical words 'jargon', dialect or slang words, or the wrong words (malapropisms).
- *Psychology* - Personality clashes, attitudes, feelings, pre-judging a situation (see also incompatible viewpoints).

Messages, Media and Channels

Why do we Communicate?

We communicate to convey ideas, feelings or both. But why do we do it? Generally we want to influence other people's understanding, attitudes or behaviour. There are four types of communication:

- Informing. This can be a combination of facts, feeling and interpretation.
- Instructing. The purpose of your instructions must be clear if you want people to change as a result.
- Motivating/persuading/encouraging. Again you want people to change their behaviour, but you may not be so confident in being able to do so - there may be opposing forces that would discourage the behaviour you wish to bring about. Instruction may not be enough; the people may need persuading to follow the instruction.
- Seeking information. This may mean you have to keep quiet and listen.

How do we Communicate?

We communicate through words, both in oral and written forms, and also without words – using signs and gestures.

Communication

Oral Communication

Speaking is the way in which most people communicate. How you speak and what you say depends on:

- who you are speaking to
- the reason
- the situation in which it takes place

For most people speaking is easy when:
- they are relaxed with their audience (friends or family)
- the subject is what they want to talk about (sport / music)
- the situation suits them (their home or a bar)

Unfortunately it isn't always possible to be in control of the factors that make speaking easy. You will have to speak to a range of people, on a range of subjects, in many different situations. Getting to know the oral skills needed for clear and effective speaking to people, known and unknown to you, is an important part of developing your communication skills.

There are many ways of communicating using the spoken word:

- Informal face-to-face conversation with a person
- Informal face-to-face conversation with a small group
- One-to-one interviewing (informal and formal)
- Formal interviewing by a panel
- A formal group meeting
- A conference presentation
- A telephone conversation with an individual
- A telephone conversation with a group – teleconferencing.

Communication

Each situation will have its own advantages and disadvantages and the chosen approach will depend very much on the situation. The advantages of talking to people rather than writing to them are:

- It can seem more natural, less formal or bureaucratic
- It can make people feel they have been personally consulted
- The sender can adjust the messages to the responses of the receiver and therefore it should mean that the message is more likely to be understood
- It is easier to express feelings as well as ideas
- It means that ideas and feelings can be easily shared
- It does allow both sender and receiver to see the 'non-verbal' communication. Even on the telephone, the tone of the voice can add to the communication.

The type of oral communication will depend on the audience and the purpose, and some examples are shown in Table 1.1.

Type of oral communication	Audience	Purpose
Interview	Prospective employer	To investigate suitability for a job
Phone call	Friend, family	Gossip and relaxed information
Phone call	Prospective customer	Sell the product
Phone call	Receptionist	To make an appointment
Tannoy	Company	Short message to company
Formal meeting	Attendees	Follow the agenda
Informal meeting	Members of the group	Catch up and information swap
Presentation	Customers, staff etc	Instruct and inform
Video	Customers and staff etc	Instruct and inform
Advert	Customers	Selling tool

Table 1.1 Types of Oral Communication, the Audience and the Purpose

Communication

There are some basic requirements for oral communication:

- *Clarity* - express your ideas clearly, speak clearly and do not try and impress people by using long and complicated words
- *Accuracy* - use the correct words to express your ideas. Avoid making statements that can't be supported.
- *Empathy* – try putting yourself in the other person's place, you don't have to agree with them, but it may help you to understand their point of view and be patient with them.
- *Sincerity* – be natural and don't put on airs and graces. Putting on an act usually means you lack confidence and can easily be detected by the listeners
- *Relax* - the best way of avoiding unnatural speech patterns is to relax.

Vocal Qualities

To produce a clear sound your jaw must not be rigid, your lips should be flexible and your throat muscles relaxed. When you are tense your vocal chords tighten and your voice becomes squeaky or shrill. You also need to control the volume and proper breathing is essential to volume control and good speaking. You can practise taking deep breaths and releasing the air with enough force to get the right volume. The volume to use will depend on the situation.

Diction and Accent – Diction is the way you pronounce words and is to some extent affected by your accent. 'Articulation' refers to the way consonants are pronounced whilst 'enunciation' refers to the way vowels are pronounced. If you mispronounce words – or drop your 't's' and 'h's' you will create a bad impression. If you have a strong regional accent you may need to lighten it slightly for people to understand you when you move out of your region.

Speed – Speaking quickly conveys a sense of urgency but it may also mean that people find it more difficult to understand what you are saying. In public speaking you will probably need to slow down – nervousness can make you speak too quickly.

Communication

Tone - Using the right tone is a valuable and necessary skill for good communication. One of your main tasks when talking with others or to an audience is to get them to listen. The tone and manner in which you speak play a major part in this. The wrong tone can distract from what you are saying.

Tone is an aspect of oral performance that is often difficult to describe, but easily felt when it is wrong or inappropriate. For example, the word "Yes" can be said in a sharp angry tone that suggests the speaker actually means "No".

Using the Telephone

As well as communicating verbally face-to-face this is also done using the telephone. The advantages of using the telephone are; it is fast, it allows you to talk even when you are unable to meet, and it removes the social and emotional distractions of a face-to-face encounter.

The first thing to remember when you are using the phone is that your listener will not see you. This means:

- You need to make it clear who you are and / or who you represent as soon as you begin.
- The normal face language of smiles, frowns, surprise, sadness has to be conveyed through your voice - mostly by tone.
- Body language such as hands, feet, etc also cannot be seen. Without these normal aids, the words you use must be precise and direct.

Expecting the Unexpected

Always prepare before you make a phone call. This means:
- Purpose - know why you are calling and what you want to say.
- Have a pen and notepaper ready for information you may receive during the call.
- Have ready any text or information - reference number, letters, memos, dates, times, calendar, diary, you think might help with certain subjects or questions if you think they are likely to arise in the discussion.
- If you happen to be calling from a mobile phone, make sure you have enough battery/credit for the call time you anticipate.

Communication

Your telephone technique

- First give your name, who you wish to speak to and the reason why you are calling.
  "Hello, this is Pauline Stone speaking, I would like to speak to Mr Rogers about a delivery of shoes that haven't arrived."

- If you have lots of information or important dates to give, ask the listener to have a pen and paper ready.
  "Have you got a pen and paper ready? I think you'll need to jot this down."
or
  " Have you got your diary at hand? I need to confirm some dates with you for our meetings next month."

- Important information or dates need to be repeated at the end of the call.
- Make sure you are talking to the right person before you begin to explain your subject in detail.
- Always speak slowly and clearly.
- If your recipient asks you to repeat what you've said, always do so willingly because:
  - they may be hard of hearing
  - while you may be able to hear them perfectly, this does not mean they can hear you with the same clarity. Learn to be sympathetic and patient.
- If you are speaking on behalf of a business or organisation, explain what your role is.

"Good morning. This is Peter Wright, technical support engineer for Mori Computers. I understand you have a problem."

Communication

Receiving Calls

Depending on the circumstances, when you receive a call give:
(a) Your number
(b) The name of the company
(c) Your name

- If you don't hear a name or any piece of information properly ask the caller to repeat it. If they are still talking too quickly or it's a bad line, ask them to spell it out. If you want to be sure, read the information back to the caller and ask them to confirm it's correct.
- If you have to take a telephone message, prepare yourself with a pen or pencil that works and plenty of paper. Be prepared to write in abbreviated note form - there is no need to write in sentences. You can re-write your notes after the call.
- When you take a call and the caller wants someone or something not at hand, don't leave them hanging on. Tell them you will ring them back.
- When you are taking a telephone message for someone else, make sure you note:
  - The caller's name and phone number
  - The message, time and date of the call

Written Communication

What a vast amount of paper would be saved if there were a law forcing writers to use only the right words [Jules Renard]

For many people, the thought of having to write a business document is enough to trigger a type of Jekyll and Hyde transformation. Over-formal words and long stilted sentences are set down in a pompous style quite unlike the writer's natural spoken manner, in the mistaken belief that 'it sounds more professional'.

Why does this happen?

Once written and sent, the message is permanent and irretrievable. It is this fact that makes us feel that we have to put painful effort into 'getting it right'. It is, of course, this very permanence that makes written communication such a useful medium; and of course great care must be taken to ensure that we are not misunderstood.

Communication

Advantages of written communication:
- It can be re-read and referred back to as often as the reader wants. It provides a means of checking back to make sure you remembered correctly.
- It is an ideal medium in which to present difficult or complex messages.
- It can be written and read when the writer and reader are in the right mood.
- Its permanence means that it can provide the basis for a legally binding agreement.
- Words can be chosen more thoughtfully and the statements can be re-shaped until you are happy with them. It allows the writer to consider, plan and check the message carefully before sending.
- You can express yourself without having to worry about the immediate response from people.
- There is physical evidence that the information was provided.
- You can send information to a number of people. It is easier and cheaper than bringing them altogether for a meeting.

There are also disadvantages
- It takes time to produce
- Feedback takes longer
- It can be less personal
- There are none of the non-verbal clues which can enhance oral communication
- It can be expensive to produce
- People don't always read written messages.

As with all communication the objective is to ensure that your written messages are:
- Received
- Understood
- Accepted
- And achieve the desired response.

The written word can be used in a variety of ways for example:
- Letters
- Reports
- Articles in journals
- Suggestions in a suggestion box
- Graffiti on walls

Communication

- Notices on a notice board
- Memos
- E-mails
- Information on Website
- Text messages
- Posters

The type of writing chosen will depend on the audience and the purpose. Some examples are given in Table 1.2.

Form of writing	Audience	Purpose
An application for a job	Employer	To get a job
A short story	Readers	To amuse or give pleasure
A newspaper article	Readers	To inform, interest or amuse
An exam paper	Students	To test ability
Instructions for using a video player	User	Instruct and inform
The Highway Code	Learner drivers	Instruct and inform
A holiday brochure	Holiday seekers	Give information and choice of holiday
A scientific paper	Peer group of scientists	To publish latest research findings
Audit report	Auditee and Management	To indicate areas of non-conformance and opportunities for improvement
Memo	Colleagues	Basic, no frills information transfer
In-house newsletter	Staff	Information, strengthen company loyalty

Table 1.2 Form of writing, its audience and purpose.

(The format for some of these forms of writing will be covered in greater detail later on in the section.)

Communication

Non-Verbal Communication

Do you think the following statements are convincing:

"He said he wasn't afraid, but I could tell from the look on his face that he was really."

"She said she really enjoyed the concert, but everybody who saw her there said she looked totally bored."

" I could tell by his eyes, he just wasn't interested."

Body language or non-verbal communication refers to the unspoken messages and signals we convey with our body. Whatever our beliefs or opinions, our emotions are usually revealed in:

- How we stand or sit
- Orientation – are we facing the person or not
- Our facial expression – a smile or a frown
- Head nods
- Hand gestures – they can emphasise our verbal message
- Appearance – grooming and choice of clothes
- Eye contact or lack of eye contact, and the length of that contact
- Body contact – the pat on the back
- Our general movements
- Proximity – the distance we are standing or sitting

Emotions are generally communicated through facial expressions. We often depend on the face to determine attitudes, since research would suggest that facial clues have considerably more focus than either verbal or other non-vocal clues.

You should be aware of the non-verbal clues you are giving as well as noticing the clues given by your receiver(s). These can give valuable insight into whether the receiver is interested and understands what you are saying. For example, a yawn is a good indicator that the message is not being well received.

Communication

A message usually has two components, the content of the message and the feeling or attitude underlying this content. Both are important and give the message a meaning. We need to be aware that voice tone or inflection, facial expression, body posture, hand and eye movements, breathing – all helps to convey the total message.

Using language and using images

The uses of language

Language has several uses. Among them are these more common ones:
- to instruct – lessons, car manual, service book, textbook, instruction leaflet.
- to amuse - jokes, stories, drama script, funny story in newspaper.
- to persuade - adverts, holiday brochure, religious leaflet.
- to inform – presentation, newspaper, magazine, notice board.
- to compare - student essay, report on products ('Which' magazine).
- to discuss - assignment, magazine article, journal.
- to reveal - news article, biography, diary, note book.

Whenever we use language it is always with some use or purpose in mind, sometimes it is obvious what we are trying to do with language. For example, an advertisement usually makes no bones about what it is trying to sell. The language the writer uses is often friendly and full of invitation, trying to convince us that 'Now is the time to buy.' This is the language of invitation or persuasion.

At other times it is not so obvious what the language is trying to do. The purpose can even be hidden. In some forms of modern advertising, the message doesn't appear to make sense until you discover it was deliberate nonsense to keep you talking and thinking about the product. 'Look out for the Surprise on 10th March'.

Language is like a multi-purpose tool that can do many jobs. Apart from the uses, there are three broad forms of language:

Functional Language - is the language we use:
- to communicate information and ideas in the work place
- for reports and business letters
- for assignments and projects

Communication

You can recognise it because it:
- is without too much description
- is organised and to the point.
- is usually factual

Personal Language - is the language we use:
- in letters to friends and family
- when we are writing about ourselves
- to give our view of an event, person or thing
- in accounts of personal experiences
- in diaries, log books and journals

You can recognise it because it:
- contains personal points of view
- is full of opinions
- relates to first hand experience

Imaginative Language - is the language we use:
- to tell stories in speech and writing
- to be adventurous with words and meanings
- for characters and situations we imagine and invent

You can recognise it because it:
- often contains detailed, colourful descriptions
- wanders off the point to explore new meaning
- is sometimes called creative writing

We will be concentrating on the use of functional writing, as this is generally the type that used in business.

Techniques for Good Business Writing

Language and Style

The language and style adopted should be plain and understandable. Outdated phrases and ungrammatical constructions are unfortunately widespread but they should be avoided at all costs. Some of the most common errors and/or bad practices, together with some suggested improvements, are given below.

Communication

Beginning and ending letters
- Many people begin letters with the phrase 'I am writing this letter to ...' This is obvious and the words should be omitted.
- If you want to begin your letter with a word ending in '...ing', take care. You must make sure that you use a complete sentence – for example, don't say 'Referring to your letter of 12 March.' A comma should follow the phrase and the sentence should be continued: 'Referring to your letter of March 12, we have now changed our records'.
- On the same principle, do not start the last sentence of your letter with a word ending in '..ing', e.g. 'Awaiting your reply'. A complete sentence should be used instead: 'I hope to hear from you soon'.

Outdated expressions
These are sometimes known as 'officialese', and are very stilted. Some examples of these expressions and their modern preferred alternatives are shown below in Table 1.3.

Not this	**But this**
We acknowledge receipt of	Thank you for
Enclosed please find Enclosed herewith Attached please find	I am enclosing
Thanking you in advance	Omit
Re	About
May we take this opportunity Allow/permit me to say	In all cases get on and do it and omit these phrases
Due to the fact that	Because/as
In the event that	If
On the occasion of	When

Table 1.3 Replacements for Out-dated Expressions

It is not good style to use as many long words as possible or to adopt a flowery or journalistic approach. The guiding principle can be summed up as follows:
>**K**eep
>**I**t
>**S**hort and
>**S**imple

Communication

To observe this principle, one discipline that can be imposed to reduce the complexity of the writing is to calculate the 'fog factor' i.e. the degree of complexity of any piece of business writing. To calculate the 'fog factor' - find the average number of words per sentence (A) and then find the average number of words per sentence with more than three syllables (B).

$$(A+B) * 0.4 = Fog\ Index$$

A fog index from 9-12 is an index of reasonable clarity. If it exceeds 12 you are placing the ideas you are trying to express under a handicap. The Bible averages 6-7, best selling books 7-8, Churchill's memorandum on report writing 7-9, a government or local government circular 23!

Engage your Reader.

Over formal writing can have the effect of distancing the writer from the reader.
Which of the following examples in Table 1.4 is more effective?

Dear Mr Carter

Your cheque was forwarded today and should be received by November 20. If it has not been received by that date, our office should be contacted on 0208 344 8831

Claims Department

Dear Mr Carter

I forwarded your cheque, today, and you should receive it by November 20. If you have not received it by that date, please contact me on 0208 344 8831

Mary Smith
Claims Adjuster

Table 1.4 Comparison of Active and Passive writing

You have probably said that the second example is more effective. This is achieved by using the active voice rather than the passive voice.

Communication

Passive vs. Active

Passive	Active
Sales meetings are held from 5.00 to 6.00pm	We hold sales meetings from 5.00 to 6.00pm

Table 1.5 Comparison of Active and Passive Writing

The messages of the Passive Voice
- It makes your writing vague
- It denies responsibility
- It creates an artificial distance between writer and reader.

The active voice inspires confidence because the reader knows who is responsible and is often more lively and interesting.

However, there are times when the Passive Voice is appropriate
- In scientific or technical writing when the actor isn't important: 'When sodium and water are combined they burn'
- In cases where tact is important: 'A serious mistake was made'

Power Verbs

'Power' verbs, are like the active voice, they say exactly what you mean to say without making your reader work harder to interpret the message.

Consider the following:

> We will do an inspection of the site on Tuesday
> vs.
> We will inspect the site on Tuesday
>
> Mr Jones makes a recommendation for buying now
> vs.
> Mr Jones recommends buying now

A **smothered verb** (the opposite of a power verb) turns the verb into a noun; it talks about acting as opposed to taking action.

Communication

A **power verb** inspires confidence, makes contact with the reader and makes your meaning plain.

Signs of smothered verbs

Smothered verbs, which have been turned into nouns, will have endings such as –ion, -tion, -ment, -ance, and -able. Try and check for these words in your writing, and see if you can turn them back into power verbs.

Avoid Classic Mistakes

Clear out negative statements
When you write in a negative rather than a positive way, you force the reader to work harder to understand your meaning.

> Example: Our insurance company will *not* pay *except* when the damage exceeds £500.
> Revised: The insurance company will pay only if the damage exceeds £500.

Readers need an additional 1/3 of a second to process each negative. Don't slow them down.

Forget 'there is' and 'there are'
When sentences start with 'there is' or 'there are', a weak sentence structure usually follows, and the real verb is not allowed to do its work. These two culprits are often followed by the word 'who'.

> Example: There are not many people who can write reports in so concise a manner
>
> Revised: Few people can write such a concise report.

Lose linking verbs
Linking verbs link subject and predicate. They lack force, energy, motion, colour and life. By using them, you often smother verbs by making them into nouns.

> Example: The company *has* two health care plans for its employees.
>
> Revised: The company *offers* its employees two health care plans.

Communication

To check your writing for linking verbs, look for *am, is, was, were, have been, has, had, seem* etc. Don't try and get rid of them all; just be aware that they can seriously weaken otherwise powerful writing.

Throw out extra verbs
The simple rule: don't use verbs you don't need.

> Example: My boss, who was a computer expert, taught me to use our system.
> Revised: My boss, a computer expert, taught me to use our system.

Don't double
Unless you have a good reason for creating emphasis, avoid using two words with the same meaning in a single sentence.

> Example: The *data* and *information* we gather will be *complete* and *comprehensive*.
>
> Revised: The data we gather will be comprehensive.

Watch weak words
When writing, avoid using the 'multiple hedge' – a string of words that create the impression you're insecure or, even worse, insincere.

> Example: It *appears* we *may possibly* be able to meet your deadline.
>
> Revised: We'll do our best to meet your deadline.

Other words to watch: perhaps, apparently, seems, generally, may, might.

Banish bias
Even the most experienced and socially aware writer must constantly work to abolish biased writing. Questions to ask:

- Is it sexist? Don't refer to all executives as men and secretaries as women.
- Is it racist? Why say that someone is black? Would you point out that someone is white?

Communication

- Is it inconsistent? Don't say 'Mr John Smith, Mr Peter Clark and Cheryl Jones volunteered.' but 'John Smith, Peter Clark and Cheryl Jones volunteered...'

Consider the Tone

As we have seen, one of the disadvantages of written communication is that, without non-verbal signals, it is much more difficult to get the right tone. Consider the following memo. Its tone is autocratic and over-formal. Would it achieve the desired results?

TO: All employees

FROM: J.B. Cox

DATE: November 6 2001

SUBJECT: Employee Punctuality

It has come to my attention that some employees are arriving later than in accordance with their scheduled starting time of 8.30am. This places an overwhelming burden on those who arrive punctually, as they must then be responsible for telephone coverage in a peak period. Your co-operation to correct this problem is appreciated. Be aware that serious repercussions may result for those who continue to abuse the system.

Communication

It could be re-written as

TO: All Employees
FROM: John Cox
DATE: November 6 2001
SUBJECT: Being on time

Although everyone should start at 8.30am, some people are arriving later than this.

We all know that phones are busy first thing in the morning. When you are late, other people must work harder to cover these calls.

We would appreciate your co-operation to put this right.

Please be on time so that there are no problems in this busy period.

Table 1.6 The effect of tone in writing

As you can see, the right tone has a huge effect on how the reader will react to the message. The golden rule is to *put yourself in the reader's shoes* – in other words, consider the receiver's likely reaction as well as what you want to achieve.

Layout and Formats

Memoranda

A memorandum, or memo, is literally a 'brief reminder'. It is used as an internal communication and should be concise and comprehensive. Many companies have their own customised memo forms or templates; others use standard printed formats.

A message headed 'Memo' or 'Memorandum' is less likely to be ignored or lost than a message just written on a plain piece of paper; it has a formality that indicates that the content is important.

'Brief' and 'concise' extend to the layout and format; there are no extras such as 'Dear….' or 'Yours…' as there would be on a business letter.

Communication

Remember, that putting something in writing makes it more lasting and often gives it more emphasis.

MEMORANDUM

To: Sonia Herson   From: Hugh Johnson
Date: 12ᵗʰ December 2001

I need to examine the stock cupboards before next Friday. Please suggest a date and time for examination.

Table 1.7 Example of a memorandum

Memorandums are being replaced by internal emails in many companies. These should follow the same rules and be clear and concise.

Business Letters

The business letter is a form of external communication, and is used as a means of confirming information, making enquiries, complaining, answering complaints, selling, advertising, tendering, giving quotations and collecting outstanding debts. It is also used as a means of conveying any type of 'one-off' message that arises as a result of day-to-day business.

The letter is often the first and only contact between an organisation and its customers, and as such conveys image and reputation. It is therefore important that it looks right, sounds right, and achieves the desired response.

Fully Blocked Layout
Most organisations these days use what is called 'fully blocked layout', in which all parts of the letter are aligned with the left hand margin. It is quick and easy to use and you do not have to worry about indenting or placing commas at the end of lines.

Communication

---

24 Fisherman's Road
Fleets Bridge
Bath
Avon
BH16 6FB

15th Jan 2002

The Service Manager
Customer Service Dept
Table Lamps Ltd
Norwich
Norfolk

Dear Sir

I am writing to enquire about a new part for my table lamp that fell off the coffee table last week. Unfortunately the switch next to the stem broke in two pieces in the fall and I was wondering if it would be possible to replace it with the same type.
I realise this....

Yours faithfully

John Scott

Table 1.8 Fully blocked layout for a letter

However, there are two other types of letter layout that, while using the same components, alter the look of the letter slightly.

Blocked
The date is near the right hand margin and the complimentary close is in the centre of the page; otherwise it is the same as for fully blocked.

Communication

Semi-blocked layout
The date and the address are in the top right-hand corner.

---

                                                          24 Fisherman's Road
                                                         Fleets Bridge
                                                         Bath
                                                         Avon
                                                         BH16 6FB

                                                         15th Jan 2002

The Service Manager
Customer Service Dept
Table Lamps Ltd
Norwich
Norfolk

Dear Sir

I am writing to enquire about a new part for my table lamp that fell off the coffee table last week. Unfortunately the switch next to the stem broke in two pieces in the fall and I was wondering if it would be possible to replace it with the same type.
I realise this....

Yours faithfully

John Scott

Table 1.9 Semi-blocked layout for a letter

Remember the only rule about using any of these formats is to be consistent. Decide on one and use it.

Communication

A word about punctuation
In business letters punctuation marks are not usually used at the end of lines of text outside the main body of the letter i.e. the references, date, receiver's name and address, salutation, complimentary close and signature block. This is referred to as 'open punctuation'. 'Closed punctuation' is the opposite – the above lines of text are punctuated normally.

House style
When it comes to layout and open or closed punctuation, all organisations have their preferred 'house style', that is the format they always use. Any business letter sent from the organisation is expected to comply with the house style.
House style will usually extend to the font style used; the usual ones are **Ariel** or **Times New Roman.**

All the principles of effective communication and the techniques you have learnt in this section apply to ensure that your letters always achieve your objective. Make sure your letters are brief, clear, helpful and positive. Avoid jargon, officialese and clichés, and always remember your receiver.

Formal Reports

Business reports play a crucial role in decision making; the more important the decision, the more likely that a report is required to aid the impartiality of the decision-making process.
Reports may be written on a routine basis, such as sales and progress reports, safety inspection reports, and so on. They may be required on an occasional basis, such as accident and disciplinary reports; or they may be especially commissioned reports, which investigate a situation and recommend future action.
The more crucial the report, the more essential it is that it should be easy to read and understand, and presented in a format that enables the reader to quickly grasp its points and conclusions. (For more details refer to the later section on 'Report Writing'.)

Communication

Using Illustrations and Images

It is said that pictures or images speak louder than words. Images with or without words can be a powerful and direct way of communicating. They can condense a large amount of information into a small space.

Images are used in communications because:
- Images are easily understood by everyone
- Images communicate ideas much quicker than words
- One image on a page is cheaper to produce than a page of words
- Images have more impact because most people prefer to spend less time reading
- Images are easy to remember

Of course, not everything can be communicated in images. Getting to know how, when and where to use images correctly are all important communication skills.

When, where and how to use Images
- Use an image only if it makes the point better than words or speech.
- Always put yourself in the position of the reader and ask yourself - is this the best way of communicating my point or my information?
- Your images should be clear and if included in a written report or assignment, should be placed near to the point they are mentioned, (or perhaps they would be better as an appendix?)
- The image should speak for itself, but you may have to introduce it or explain its relevance.
- Keep your images as simple as possible. Do not try to convey too much information in one image.
- Always use a title, heading or caption above or below your image so that the audience can tell at a glance what it shows.
- In the case of a written report or assignment, keep your image to a sensible scale so that it can be understood easily.
- In the planning stage of reports or assignments ask yourself - is there scope here for an image or illustration? If so, then what kind?

Communication

In written work it is possible to have a range of images to help communicate your ideas. The range of possible images includes:

Photographs

A good photograph will give an excellent image of the object but it can be difficult to light correctly and some level of expertise is needed.

Diagrams and sketches

There are a variety of diagrams that can be used to present information. An orthographic drawing is made up of the back, front and sides elevations of an object and it must be drawn to scale. It is most useful for designers and manufacturers. An isometric drawing provides a pictorial method of showing something. It lacks perspective and so can look odd. A perspective drawing includes perspective and looks more natural, but it is more difficult to draw. An exploded drawing shows how something is put together by pulling apart the object into its constituent parts. A cutaway drawing shows an object with part of the cover removed. A sketch is an informal diagram.

Flow charts

A flow chart is a diagrammatic representation of the sequence of operations in a process. There is a standard set of symbols for using in these charts and software is available to help draw them. An example flow chart is shown in Figure 1.2.

Communication

Preparing a Talk

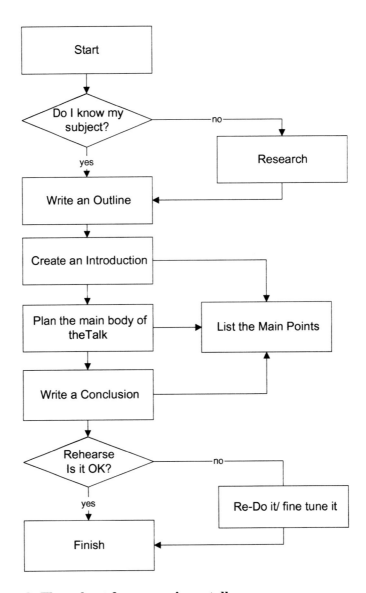

Figure 1.2 Example Flow chart for preparing a talk

Communication

Organisational chart

This type of chart shows the organisational hierarchy of an organisation and an example is shown in Figure 1.3

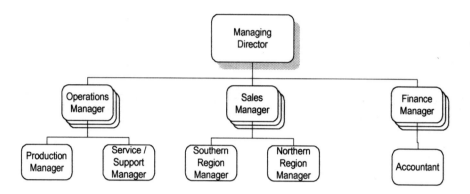

Figure 1.3 Example Organisation Chart

Maps and Plans

If you use maps or plans in a report you must add a scale and it is also useful to show north on a map as a small arrow.

Graphs, Charts and Tables

Written work may also include images such as graphs, charts and tables which are used for presenting data and these are covered in Section 2.

Visual Aids

As well as written work, images are useful in discussions and oral presentations. In this case visual aids will be required.
For example:
- Large Posters or Flip Charts.
- Video & TV screen to show moving images.
- Chalkboard or Whiteboard for any form of chart, diagram or illustration.
- OHP (Over head Projector) for images prepared in advance like maps, detailed diagrams etc. The information can be slowly revealed in sequence.

Communication

- Slides for still images that can be enlarged for general classroom viewing. Readily available slides are easy to get for most subjects, and it is possible to produce your own slides without too much extra expense. There are now electronic projectors, which allow slides to be assembled on the computer and displayed straight from it.
- Photocopied images or illustrations provide your audience with permanent reference material during your talk.
- Computers (particularly those with a CD-ROM drive) can provide high quality still or moving images to support a talk or discussion.

(The use of images in presentations will be covered in more detail in Section 2.)

Remember, before you use an image in either written or oral work you have to decide why you are using it and what purpose it will serve.

Will it:
- Display information or offer a quick summary
- Show some kind of comparison (e.g. Bar or line graph, pie chart)
- Show details about a machine, object or process (e.g. diagram or flow chart)
- Create an impression or cause an emotional reaction (e.g. photograph -black or white or full colour?)
- Serve as an introduction, summary or end to a report (e.g. photograph, chart or diagram).
- Introduce new / old information in a better way
- Help others to understand your subject.

Powers of Persuasion, Motivation and Change

As we identified earlier some of the reasons for communicating are to persuade, influence, motivate and hopefully achieve a change in behaviour – but how is this achieved? If you are trying to do this it will usually mean changing the beliefs, attitudes or behaviour of the recipient. You may need to present a case, a report or an argument in favour of or against a situation. You need to recognise how difficult a task this is. You will have to appeal to both the heart and head of your audience. This is achieved by referencing the benefits of your case with evidence to support your position. This evidence could be statistics, authoritative opinions, the experience of others – but whatever you choose it must be relevant and accurate. Try not to generalise or exaggerate and avoid using 'emotive' and coloured language. If your

Communication

argument is based on assumptions then make sure you explain them. If you have your own prejudices try not to show them. If this is not possible admit them or make sure you give some references to the other side of the story.

Your structure must be **very** logical – and inductive order can be very persuasive. You must
- Grab the audience's attention
- Find out what the audience's interests and requirements are
- Demonstrate how you can meet these requirements
- Get them to agree

The structure of a document is also important when your purpose is to persuade.

The two main purposes of a management document are either to inform or to inform and persuade.

For informing then the material needs to be laid out in a simple way that conveys information clearly, and the chance of confusion is low – choose a logical sequence e.g. chronological, geographical, order of importance. However, when you are trying to persuade, then the structure should lead the reader towards the conclusions and recommendations that you want them to agree to. In management writing this is usually achieved through the power of reasoning and logic. The document should be structured in such a way that it helps the logic and reasoning to emerge very clearly. A logical structure that could be used is:
- Statement of problem
- Analysis of problem
- Possible solutions
- Recommended solution

or
- Proposition
- Evidence
- Conclusion
- Recommended course of action

Communication

or
- Proposal for action
- Need for action
- Possible problems
- Expected benefits
- Conclusions
- Recommendations

There are several basic formats that can be used to meet particular needs.

Report
    What happened in a logical order?
    Conclusion
    What should be done?

A progress report
    What has happened so far?
    What still needs to be done?
    Any problems that remain in completing the task
    The solutions to these problems
    What should be done?

A position paper
    The current position (policy)
    The reasons why the policy needs to change (changing circumstances, environment etc)
    Requirements of the new policy
    Recommendations for changes to the policy

When you wish to set out the options and in a way that will lead to a particular option being chosen, then it is more effective to begin with the weaker option (in your opinion) and progress to the strongest. Thus if there were several courses of action, start with the least desirable and eliminate it by setting out conclusive arguments against it, then move to the next option and eliminate it; until finally when you reach the desired option it will seem obvious that this is the most suitable solution.

Communication

Your writing or presenting will be strengthened if you never present opinions as facts. All statements of opinion should where possible, be based on factual evidence contained in the paper or supported by reference to an external, well-respected authority. The same is true of conclusions. Unless you have supporting evidence, opinions and conclusions are just your assertions and will be challenged and contradicted.

Active Listening

Active listening is an important skill in persuasion and it is an important way to bring about change in people. Sensitive listening is a most effective agent for individual personality change and development of a group. Listening can bring about changes in people's attitudes towards themselves and others and then bring about changes in basic values and personal philosophy.

People who have been listened to in an 'active' way become more emotionally mature, more open to their experiences, less defensive, more democratic and less authoritarian.

If you listen to people carefully and sensitively, then they are more likely to listen to others in this manner and this means groups of good listeners tend to be less argumentative and more likely to work together, with everyone feeling that they have made a worthwhile contribution.

Section 2

The Organisational Dimension

The Organisational Dimension

The Organisational Dimension

Information Gathering and Research Activities

Information Gathering

There are four main sources of information:

- *People* e.g. colleagues, politicians, manufacturers, retailers, federations, unions, and pressure groups.
- *Books and other publications* e.g. reference books, text books, guides, handbooks, journals and magazines, newspapers, maps and charts, previous reports.
- *Information technology and the media*. The growth of the Internet and the World Wide Web has provided access to a vast array of information including on-line databases, on-line library catalogues, bulletin boards and topic groups. The modern search engines can provide a huge range of possible sites to visit.
- *Events and places* e.g. libraries, laboratories, research institutions, exhibitions, museums, galleries, talks.

Information can be gathered in various ways:

- *Desk Research* - used for gathering facts from books, magazines, newspapers, and journals and the World Wide Web. When reading skim the article first and see if it is suitable (that is the right level, current etc). If it is helpful then read it carefully and make notes.
- *Experimentation* – usually used by scientists to test out ideas, but can be used on other occasions. The write up of the experiment should include the objective of the experiment, the theory underlying the experiment, a description of how the experiment was carried out, the results and a statement of the final results including assumptions and possible error bars.
- *Listening* – to a speaker, the radio etc. Listen effectively and examine the evidence presented, is it accurate and complete or are there weaknesses? Make notes – this can help you concentrate. However, do not let the note-taking take over the listening and understanding.
- *Observe* – look and see what happens if you are interested in an activity. You can learn a great deal by seeing what actually happens – it may not be the same as what the people doing the activity report.

The Organisational Dimension

- *Interview* – this is not an easy task but is essential when you need to find out about attitudes, feelings and emotions. Market research companies trying to gauge public opinion often use interviews. Care must be taken in the phrasing of questions – they can lead to a biased response.
- *Letter* – this can be sent to ask for information, in this case it is usually polite to enclose a self-addressed envelope. If you are asking for information in the letter, it must be clear what information you need. When writing 'request for information' letters follow the rules set out in Table 2.1.

DON'T	DO
Ask for confidential information	Make the letter easy to understand
Ask people to do research work for you	Send it to the right person
Expect people to answer your questions immediately	Ask a few specific questions
Make a pest of yourself by continually asking questions	Realise they are doing you a favour

Table 2.1 Do's and Don'ts when requesting information

- *Telephone* – this is useful for collecting simple and short information. Long complex information is difficult to collect in this manner and another approach should be used. When using the telephone to collect data then check first that you are talking to the right person and it is often useful to have your questions jotted down so that nothing is forgotten.
- *Accessing* – Using the worldwide web. Use the commercial search engines – but take care, you can generate more data than you can deal with. It can be very time-consuming to sift through the websites and so try and use the advanced features of the search engines to narrow down the results.
- *Questionnaire* – this can be used to gain information from or the opinion of a sample of people. Check that the data you seek has not already been collected and that using a questionnaire is the most appropriate method. Using tick boxes for answers makes it easier for the respondent and it will make it easier for you to process. The questionnaire should be straight forward for you to analyse and where possible it should be 'pilot tested' among a small group of respondents to iron out any problems.

The Organisational Dimension

Creating a Questionnaire

Generally there are four elements to the creation of a questionnaire:
1. *The questions to be used.* The questions should be clear, unambiguous, short and to the point. There should only be one issue per question. The format of the questions is important and in certain circumstance it may be necessary to make the questions positive, not negative. If the questions are negative, the questionnaire may emphasise the bad points instead of building on the good.

Negative: What do you dislike about our service?
Positive: What do you like about our service?

2. *The response format.* E.g. multiple choice, written response, scoring (like to dislike using the scale 1 to 5), yes/no.
3. *Introduction to the questionnaire.* E.g. "As a valued and trusted customer you have been selected as.........." followed by an explanation of the questionnaire's aims and objectives, the benefits in completion, confidentially, analysis of the results, time to complete etc.
4. *Final review of the completed questionnaire* – its look and feel. Getting the right impression of the questionnaire is important in obtaining the correct level of response. This means considering Desk Top Publishing, proof reading, length, question style etc.

Sampling - distribution of the questionnaire

The questionnaires are unlikely to be sent to every possible target and so some form of representative sampling will need to be completed.

Sampling methods include:
- The whole of the database (OK with a small number of targets).
- Statistical sampling: random or stratified e.g. income, age range, gender, or cluster - from a particular geographical location or office.

The Organisational Dimension

Obtaining a response

Consideration needs to be given to the manner in which the information is obtained.
Posting the response is an obvious option, but there are problems with this. Will the questionnaire be completed? Will the questions be understood? Will a response be obtained from the most valuable targets? However, using the post will speed up the data gathering exercise.

Another option is having face-to-face discussions with the target. Although, this could be a less efficient way of gathering the information, it may be an important marketing and personal relationship exercise that provides more information than a questionnaire.
If the service person, (possibly the service engineer) has the face-to-face discussions with the target, this may be an opportunity for the service provider and the target to see the service person's role in a different light, extending the their role and the service provided.

The response rate from questionnaires is not good; typically a ten percent return is excellent. To improve on this return ratio there are some methods to cajole the target into responding:
- An incentive - enter into a prize draw.
- Reason for the questionnaire - how it will help improve the service.
- Ease of return; email, prepaid reply envelope, etc.
- Use an impartial third party.

EXAMPLE An internal questionnaire to determine the value of the Quality Management System in a Project Management Organisation

Introduction

You have been specially selected to assist in assessment of the capability of our organisation's Project Control related processes. The objective of this questionnaire is to provide information regarding our capability in managing projects and satisfying the customer's needs. The information will also provide an indication of areas or projects that require greater focus in a subsequent in-depth assessment.

Please answer the following questions in relation to recent experience within the organisation, so that the information may be used to gain an overall impression of the current project management processes used.

The Organisational Dimension

The information will be kept confidential to the assessment team, only the analysis of all questionnaires will be reported and reporting will be non-attributable to individuals.

Do not spend too long answering any one question. If you don't know what the question is asking, just leave it and move on to the next. The whole questionnaire should take less than 20 minutes to complete. If you have any difficulties, or it is taking significantly longer than 20 minutes, please contact the Quality Department.

Please return the completed questionnaire to the Quality Department.

Statement	Regarding your role and responsibility do you				
	Strongly Agree	Agree	Disagree	Strongly Disagree	Not Know
Documented procedures (quality manual) accurately reflect what actually happens on a project.	☐	☐	☐	☐	☐
We satisfactorily control customer specifications.	☐	☐	☐	☐	☐
The team's tasks are clearly defined in the Project Handbook.	☐	☐	☐	☐	☐
Only projects with strong Project Leaders will succeed.	☐	☐	☐	☐	☐
Data is regularly provided on completion of tasks.	☐	☐	☐	☐	☐
Design and project reviews take place, and minuted actions agreed.	☐	☐	☐	☐	☐
It does not matter which project I work on, the process is still the same.	☐	☐	☐	☐	☐
Bad news is always transmitted to the customer.	☐	☐	☐	☐	☐
Data from previous projects is readily available when making estimates.	☐	☐	☐	☐	☐
The quality of the customer deliverables is consistently good.	☐	☐	☐	☐	☐
Number and severity of faults or errors identified on all projects can be tracked.	☐	☐	☐	☐	☐
We know when a project is going wrong by analysing the project data.	☐	☐	☐	☐	☐
Project progress can be determined by reference to the project programme.	☐	☐	☐	☐	☐
Methods such as Contract Review are used to assess the quality of the customer's requirements.	☐	☐	☐	☐	☐
Communication routes are well understood, used and managed?	☐	☐	☐	☐	☐

The Organisational Dimension

Customer's preference or other pressures cause 'Quality' practices to be compromised.	☐	☐	☐	☐	☐
Our organisation and projects suffer from 'initiative fatigue'.	☐	☐	☐	☐	☐
We have adequate project resources.	☐	☐	☐	☐	☐
Plans are reviewed and updated on a regular basis.	☐	☐	☐	☐	☐
When things sometimes go wrong, someone is always held accountable.	☐	☐	☐	☐	☐
Our estimates accurately reflect the actual time and effort spent on projects.	☐	☐	☐	☐	☐
Where training is required it is provided.	☐	☐	☐	☐	☐
The risks we face are addressed in the planning stage of the project.	☐	☐	☐	☐	☐
Customer coordination is well managed.	☐	☐	☐	☐	☐
Interfaces e.g. Inter Office, Suppliers, Contractors, etc. is well managed.	☐	☐	☐	☐	☐

Literature Surveys

A literature survey is a specialist form of information gathering that tends to be used for major research reports such as theses. Prior to beginning a project (and during, if new facts are uncovered), survey (read) the available literature on the subject. This is to see if other researchers have covered similar topics to you or have already solved your problem. It will also give you the authoritative references you need to support your own conclusions and may help form and direct your own approach. For instance, for a project on customer satisfaction you could read about the experiences of others in measuring customer satisfaction. It may point to techniques that work best in certain situations. This reference can then be used to support the choice of this technique in the project. In general, you are looking to see if other people have experienced similar situations and whether their results can throw illumination on your problem. Reading around your subject should help you design a better approach to methodology, let you benefit from the experience of others and shorten your learning curve.
The references must be acknowledged in the text. You should use the Harvard System of referencing. When you base some text on somebody else's work or you quote from their work, you must acknowledge your source. In the Harvard system this is done by putting the author's surname, the date of publication and the pages referred to in brackets after a quotation as follows: (Tickle & Vorley, 1999:54). If you are summarising their work, you must insert the author's surname and the date of publication: (Tickle &Vorley, 1999). When you include the author's name in a sentence then you

The Organisational Dimension

can put the date in brackets after it: "Tickle & Vorley (1999) suggested that...."

The bibliography at the back of the report must contain the full details of the text you are referring to:

> Tickle & Vorley (1999) Fred Tickle and Geoff Vorley *Introduction to Quality Assurance* 1st Ed Quality Management and Training (Publications) (1999)

If the reference is to a Journal then it should be written:

> Name of Author, year, title of contribution, *in* name of journal, volume number, part number, page numbers.

When you reference a newspaper article the format is:

> Name of writer, year, title of article, name of paper, date (minus year), page number

TV and radio programmes are references as follows:

> Title of programme, episode number, title of episode, transmitting organisation, channel, full date (Year, Month, Day), time of transmission

For www pages that are referenced, the format is:

> Constructor (person or organisation), year, title of page or site, date created or update, URL, date accessed

For example

> Quality Management and Training (2000) October Newsletter (updated 6 October 2001) http:www.qmt.co.uk/newsletter/October.htm, (accessed 6 November 2002)

The Organisational Dimension

Recording and sorting your findings

In some organisations you will have to maintain your working papers as backup to your work, and so how you record your findings needs to be well structured. Whenever you gather information, it is important to keep a note of where, when and from whom or what your information comes from. This enables you to:
- Explain your sources of information
- Check one source against another
- Return to a source for further information or checking

If the information required has been well planned, then the sorting is straightforward and you follow the heading and subheading layout planned for the final presentation of your work.

Once you have organised your information you need to study your material for anything important that may have been left out. To do this effectively you should use a checklist. Can you:
- make clear the terms of reference
- produce a relevant and precise title
- write an introduction which clarifies the background, purpose, audience and structure
- comment on your method
- state the limitations
- decide on your findings

Once you have gathered all you information, you will need to consider how reliable it is and how significant it is.

There are several factors that can be used to judge the reliability of the information. *Accuracy* – Can the data be checked? Are the calculations correct? Is it out of date? *Objectivity* – Have all the major points of view been fairly represented? Don't use statements without supporting evidence. *Completeness* – It is difficult to prove that all the information has been found, but check that you have provided all the relevant information and whether any attempt to mislead or deceive has been made through omission of any data. And finally *Strength* – The evidence is strong when it can be verified or re-performed, several sources have reached the same conclusion and it agrees with the general body of knowledge.

The Organisational Dimension

To judge the significance of your findings you must try and step back from them and assess the implications of what you have found. What is the most significant finding? Do not just list everything you have found with the same level of importance. Prioritise your findings – the priority should reflect the requirements of the reader and not you. You may have found some nuance in experimentation that you find fascinating, but the readers are interested in the results and not necessarily the technical details.

Check your findings, if there are areas that have gaps it is better to go back and fill them now, rather than be asked about it after the report has been issued.

There are some skills that will help you in gathering data.

Reading Efficiently

Scan the information you have found for key words to see if the article or paper is useful.
Sort your reading into:
- Quick reading to get a general background.
- Careful reading (notes can help you concentrate and remind you of the points to make).
- Information that is unhelpful and so you should not waste time reading it.

Faster reading can usually be achieved by:
- Concentration
- Taking in phrases rather than just words
- Forcing the pace by moving your finger quickly down the page and trying to keep up
- Do not mouth or vocalise the words

Note taking

Make notes as you go through the material. The most important thing to remember in note taking is the value of space. Do not cramp your notes – leave plenty of room for future comments. There are two basic methods of note taking - traditional notes and patterned notes.

In traditional notes the material is structured using headings and subheadings. Use double spacing and only write on one side of the paper. This allows you to add additional notes as you go.

The Organisational Dimension

Pattern notes use an approach that allows you to summarize your understanding and find links between ideas and information. Starting at the centre of the page the ideas and notes spray out from it. An example of patterned notes using a spider diagram method is given in Figure 2.1.

The advantages of using patterned notes are:
- You can see an overview of the topic
- It is easy to add to them
- Links can be highlighted
- You can see more easily where additional information is needed
- They are quicker to write

The disadvantage is that they can become very complex and they are not suitable for noting down just facts or lists of information.

The Organisational Dimension

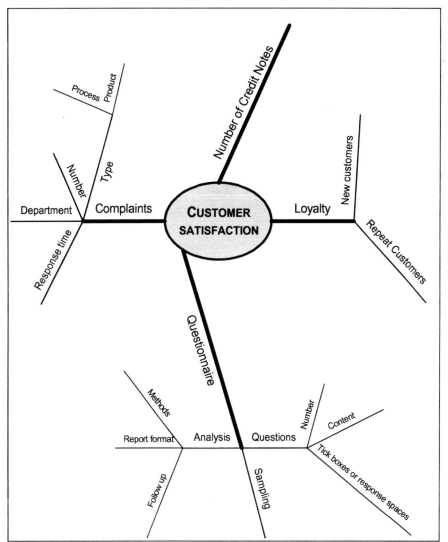

Figure 2.1 An example of a Spider Diagram used for Note taking

You can use both approaches at once. When note taking, have a double page to write on. Use the left hand side to draw pattern information and the right hand side for more linear information. Key words and phrases will usually be all that are needed and these can be recorded in a pattern to show how they link together. This is often a more effective approach than trying to write everything down.

The Organisational Dimension

Analysis and Presentation of Data
Qualitative and Quantitative Data

It is often assumed that figures speak for themselves. This is rarely the case. Generally you have to interpret figures and hunt for meaning. It is essential to 'polish' figures as you do words and to choose the most effective way of communicating them so that the recipients draw the conclusions that you want them to draw.

Quantitative data is numerical data e.g. measurements of temperature, voltage. To plot histograms or pie charts etc. this type of data has to be divided into classes e.g. the temperature measured is on a continuous scale and so to plot this you would need to divide into classes ($10 - 20°C$, $21 - 30°C$). Qualitative data is not numerical, but records an attribute or a quality and is in classes or categories already. This type of data is sometimes called categorical data. Examples of such qualitative data are; nationalities of students in a class, types of car people drive, responses to a survey requesting opinions. In both types of data, the number of items in each class is called the frequency and the proportion of data items in each class, the relative frequencies.

There are a variety of ways of analysing and presenting qualitative and quantitative data.

Bar Chart

This is a way of presenting one-dimensional data; there are no dependent or independent variables. A bar chart is not a very useful tool for interpreting data, but it can be quite an effective way of presenting information visually. It provides a simple way of comparing values by using bars of different lengths.

The Organisational Dimension

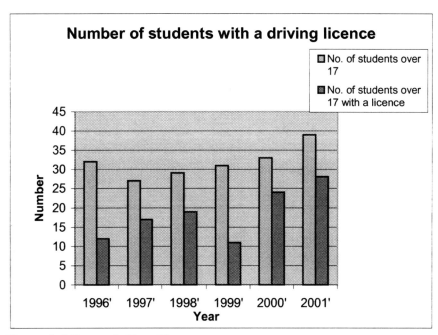

Figure 2.2 Example Bar Chart

There are variations on the bar chart – sectional bar charts show the magnitude of items and their constituent parts. Percentage bar charts show the percentage a constituent part bears to the whole. Dual bar charts compare two or more related quantities over time, as seen in Figure 2.2.

The Organisational Dimension

A pictogram is similar to a bar chart except that it uses symbols instead of bars to represent magnitudes or frequencies.

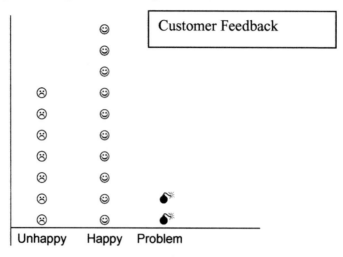

Figure 2.3 Example Pictogram showing customer feedback results

Histogram

The histogram is a neat way of setting out data into a pictorial representation that reveals the shape of the distribution.
The histogram is a series of bar charts placed beside each other for comparison. The audience or reader can see a trend for each category over a period of time. A three-dimensional effect is easily obtained with computer graphics.

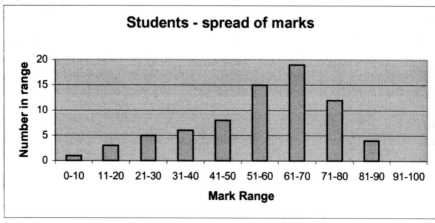

Figure 2.4 Example histogram showing the spread of student marks

The Organisational Dimension

Table

If you are using a table make sure that the figures are correct and restrict figures to those that are meaningful. If you have a lot of tables to include, then you should consider putting them into the Appendices.

Statistical tables usually show how one thing is related to another – and may be described as 'two dimensional'. Often the broad patterns and significant features are obscured by excessive detail and poor layout.
- Is the table a jumble of figures? – then try reducing the number of digits, rounding the numbers, using better spacing and layout.
- Is there any logic in ordering the rows or numbers?
- Is it difficult to compare figures? – try interchanging rows and columns.
- Would it help to find row or column averages?
- Would it help to convert to percentages?
- What other information is needed?

Even when a table has been simplified it still may not be the best approach to presenting figures.

Graphs

A graph can deal with 2 distinct dimensions at the same time and can give a very clear overview of the data. The convention is to use the horizontal axis for the independent variable. A graph can provide a 'picture' of patterns and trends. It can reveal regular or unexpected fluctuations and can be helpful for projecting trends into the future. Where appropriate, error bars must be included.

If you are doing an experiment, it is useful to draw a rough graph as you go along, then if there are any irregularities you can go back and check them.

When drawing a graph choose a scale in which the lines or curve will take up most of the graph. However, be careful about misleading people. If you do not choose the scale to start at zero then it can give an incorrect impression of the variations. Also if you miss out sections of the data then the evidence can be misleading. An example graph is shown in Figure 2.5.

The Organisational Dimension

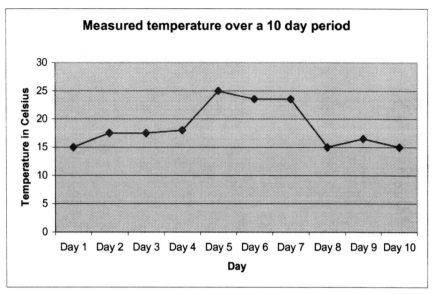

Figure 2.5 Example graph showing temperature variation

Pie Chart

A pie chart is a circle divided by radii into sectors whose areas are proportional to the relative magnitudes or frequencies of the set of items. It is a good way of showing relative proportions. An example is shown in Figure 2.6

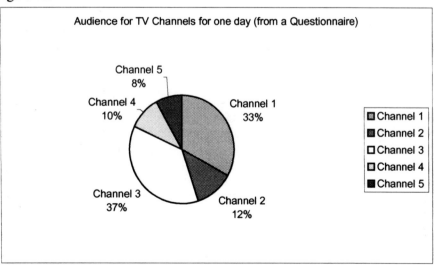

Figure 2.6 Example pie chart showing the distribution of TV audiences

The Organisational Dimension

Report Writing

A report is the communication of information or advice from the person who has gathered data and facts, to the person who requested the report. Reports are often used to provide a basis for decisions or actions.

Preparation

Before you start writing your report you must ask yourself some questions. The answers to these will help you decide on the structure and content of the report such that it meets the requirements of the reader.
- What are the general aims of the report?
- What is the subject of the report?
- How much information should go into the report?
- What form of report is required?
- What resources do you have at your disposal? (How many hours can you allocate to it, what is the budget, do you need any equipment?)
- Who will read the report? Who are the primary and secondary readers?
- To whom will you submit the final report?
- By when must the report be finished?
- What do the readers need to know about the subject? Do the needs of the primary and secondary readers differ?
- Any special considerations to be borne in mind?
- What response is required from the readers? To what use will they put the information in the report?
- What kind of relationship do you wish to establish between you and your readers?

If your readership is mixed then you may need to look at structuring the report to meet the different needs of the readers, e.g. a summary for the chief executive, the main body of the work for the managers and appendices with detailed technical information for the research and development department.

The objectives of the report should be clear in your mind. They should be stated as clearly, concisely and accurately as possible in terms of the results to be achieved by the report. You should use this to set yourself objectives against which you can measure your own performance.

The Organisational Dimension

Initial Framework

This is the plan and allows you to gain an overview of the entire report. It highlights the information that needs to be collected and helps maintain the perspective of the report whilst gathering information. This framework will be influenced by the needs of the person who requested the report, the house style, custom, conventions and your objectives. Take care while planning the structure, as a suitable structure will allow everything else to fall into place. Do not forget that people tend to remember what they read first and last more than what they read in the middle.

All reports have a set of typical components:

Title page
> Title
> The name and position of the person who requested (authorised) the report
> Author (name and position)
> Organisation name
> Date issued
> Reference number
> Confidentiality level and distribution list

Forward
> This is not generally found in reports. However if required it would be written by a third party as an introduction to the work

Preface
> It is used by a writer to tell the reader some personal background information behind the document – again this is not generally found in reports.

Acknowledgements
> This section is used by the author to thank people who have helped in the report preparation.

Contents
> A contents page is needed for any report more than a few pages long. Make sure the headings on the content page are the same as those in the report. Word Processing packages can produce this for you

The Organisational Dimension

Summary or Abstract
> This is a key section and is often the only part of the report read by management! The summary must highlight the key facts, the main conclusions and recommendations. It is usually written last and should never cover anything that is not already in the report.

Introduction
> This section must set out the main aims and objectives of the report. It must also raise people's interest and set the scene for the main body of the report. It may include information on why the report was written, the resources available, any limitations, and the type of information sources used.

Methodology
> The methods used to gather the data. It should explain why and how you went about gathering the information needed to meet the objectives of the report.

Results and Analysis
> The results you have obtained presented in the most appropriate way. You should include the analysis of the data received using the methods described in your methodology. (See section on Analysis and Presentation of data for further information.)

Conclusions
> The conclusions should refer back to the objectives set out at the beginning of the report and should flow from the findings and analysis presented in the main body of the report.

Recommendations
> Only make recommendations if you were asked to do so by the report's requester. Recommendations should look forward, they should not comment on the past or present (this can be done in the conclusions).

The Organisational Dimension

Appendices
> Appendices allow you to supplement the information given in the main text. They provide added detail for the readers who are interested without making the main text too long and difficult to follow. They can also contain documentary evidence to support arguments presented in the main body e.g. memos, faxes, and letters. Appendices must be clearly referred to in the main body of the report so that the reader knows they are there.

References
> This section should list the books or journals that have been specifically mentioned or quoted in the text. The list should be in the order the books were referenced.

Bibliography
> This also gives full details of every publication, but unlike a reference section may include books and journals not referenced but that provide additional reading for the subject. It is customary to list them alphabetically by the author's surname.

Glossary
> This is helpful if you are using specialised vocabulary. Make sure that the definitions are correct and up to date. If a large number of your readership is unfamiliar with the vocabulary then this section can be placed near the beginning.

Index
> This is only necessary for a large report. List items alphabetically and two columns are often used to present the information. Most word processing packages will have methods that allow indexes to be easily produced.

Collecting and Handling Information

The framework you developed for the report will have identified the information you need to collect. It is better to collect more information than you need, as it is easier to write if you have lots to choose from. (How to gather information was covered in an earlier section). Don't forget to refer back to the objectives, terms of reference and readership to make sure that you cover all angles.

The Organisational Dimension

To help you decide whether you are ready to start writing ask yourself the following:
- Have you consulted all sources of information?
- Are your notes sufficiently detailed on each aspect of the subject?
- Have you checked your preparation against your terms of reference, readership analysis and objectives?

The components that should be drafted first are the main body and the appendices. You don't have to start at the beginning, choose a subsection or appendix that you feel most confident about – this will lead you in gently. Once you have written the main body, leave it for a time and then when you come back to re-read it put yourself in the reader's mind. Does it say what you wanted it to say?

As you read the draft check:
- Is the structure logical? Is it the best way of presenting your facts and arguments?
- Is the tone correct for the audience?
- Are your figures, calculations, spelling and grammar correct?

After the main body and appendices have been re-drafted to your satisfaction then you can move on to writing the conclusions, recommendations (if required), introduction and summary.

At this point try and leave it for a few days, or at least several hours. When you return to re-read it check that it flows, that there are adequate signposts and links for the reader to follow through the report and understand the conclusions and recommendations you have written. Make sure that there is nothing you would not be willing to stand up and say. Following any necessary re-drafts - if possible get other people (colleague, line manager etc) to read it - can they follow the report? What comments do they have? You may also wish to give it to somebody else (non-technical) just to proof read it for spelling and grammar. Colleagues may not have seen errors in these, as they will have concentrated on the technical information.

The Organisational Dimension

Final Version

Following the checking and comments it is then possible to complete the final version and issue it. Organisations have their own policies for issuing reports and it may include a formal presentation.

Report Style

The above section considered the practicalities of report writing, however, you also need to consider the style of the writing. It is not possible to define a good writing style since everyone will have his or her own style to a certain extent. However, a good style in business communication should combine clarity, conciseness and directness. The style should be unobtrusive, it should not interfere with the technical content of the report and it should be easy to read. (See the section on good business writing for more details).

In summary:
- Omit unnecessary words from sentences
- Do not include superfluous material
- Use direct statements with active verbs in preference to the passive voice
- Keep sentences short
- Change long words and phrases to shorter ones where possible
- Make sure you know the exact meaning of the words you use and use them in the appropriate context
- Each sentence should have one subject and each paragraph should deal with a single topic
- Check that everything you write is accurate, all facts should be verifiable. An incorrect fact can mean that the whole report loses its credibility.

The Organisational Dimension

Report Presentation

A report should be presented to attract and gain the attention of the readers. It should also allow them to find their way through it easily and pick out any particular section that interests them. The appearance of the report is often dictated by house style that will define the font, layout and general presentation with the organisation's own cover sheets. If you have free-reign to present a report then take care to make it consistent and suitable for the subject. A technical report on production quality problems would not be suitable for the same flamboyance of presentation that a design student may use for an end of year fashion presentation.

Headings and Subheadings

People find it easier to read if the text is broken up into blocks. Headings and subheadings label these blocks of type. Once you have started a topic with a heading or subheading you must not change to another topic until another heading or subheading is provided. Subheadings should not repeat the information in the heading. There are no standard headings or subheadings but they should be short, easily interpreted, and should not overlap. They should be in a logical order and should not be vague e.g. general, others.

Numbering

Report pages should always be numbered for ease, index and reference purposes. The sections can also be numbered e.g. 1, 1.1, 1.1.1. Do not go beyond three levels of numbering; instead look at re-structuring the section.

Highlighting

If you wish to highlight areas of the text there are several ways that this can be done. Using CAPITALS, using **BOLD,** underlining or *Italic fonts* and by using indents and bullets. What ever you use do not overdo it and keep to the same method throughout the report.

The Organisational Dimension

Illustrations

Illustrations that are well produced and appropriate can enhance a report. When using an image in a report it should have a caption and a figure number. Where appropriate you must acknowledge the source. You should discuss the figure in the text and make sure it shows what you intended it to show. Using too many illustrations can overwhelm the reader and cause them to lose the thread of the report.

Paper, Cover and Bindings

This may also be prescribed by the organisation. Most reports are written on white A4 paper of a reasonable quality. Every report should have covers, even if it is only an extra piece of paper back and front. When choosing the colour of the covers consider that dark colours are often depressing and light colours can give the impression of light-heartedness. Safe colours for reports are blue and green.

The type of binding will depend on the size of the report and the expense you wish to go to. It will also depend on whether you wish to add or amend things at a later date and so will need to undo the binding. Simple methods include stapling, plastic gripper, ring binding, and gluing and stitching (for larger reports).

Making Presentations

Preparation for Communicating

Why?
What is the purpose of the communication? What am I trying to achieve? What do I want the receiver(s) to do following the communication? Am I trying to inform, persuade, educate, entertain ....?

Who?
Who are the audience? What sort of people are they? At what level does my message need to be for them to understand it? How much do they already know about my subject?

The Organisational Dimension

Where and When?
Where will the audience be when they get my message? Will they be distracted or prepared? Is my communication in response to a question of theirs? In this case they will be ready and interested in the answer.

What?
What do I want to say? What do I need to say? What do they need to know? What information must I include in order to be - Clear – Concise – Courteous – Constructive – Correct and Complete?

How?
How will I communicate, with words, pictures or both? What sort of presentation shall I give?

Planning the Message

Once you have decided why you want to communicate, whom you are going to communicate to, where and when you are going to communicate, what you are going to say and how you are going to say it, then you need to plan the message.

- *Write down your purpose.* In one or two sentences write down what you are trying to achieve with this presentation. Get your objectives clear – are you trying to persuade, inform or educate your audience?
- *Know the audience you are speaking to* This allows you to gauge the level of detail to use. Think of the difference in speaking to a high school on sales and marketing and a group of sales personnel.
- *Assemble the information.* Use notes to jot down all the ideas and points you wish to make. Ask yourself whether the information is relevant to the talk and the audience, if not then leave it out. Make sure you know your subject and all the relevant details.
- *Group the information.* Take your notes, look for links and place them in groups.
- *Put the information into a logical sequence.* Put your groups of information into a logical order that the audience can follow. The most commonly used methods of ordering material are:
  - *Chronological order* – present the material in order of the time that it occurred
  - *Spatial (or place) order* – this is useful for furniture, buildings etc. For instance, the facts are presented in geographical location – and ordered from north to south for instance

The Organisational Dimension

- *Order of importance* – you can start with the most important point first to gain attention or build up to the most important point to increase anticipation. In business it is usually advisable to start with the most important point.
- *Ascending order of complexity* – presenting the simple ideas first and building upon them to the more complex ideas.
- *Descending order of familiarity* – starting with a known idea and building upon it towards the unfamiliar ideas.
- *Cause and effect* – this happened and so that happened
- *Topical* – if there is no real link between the groups then cover the information topic by topic

- *Produce a skeleton outline.* Producing this outline can help identify missing links or where the notes are too complex.
- *Write the first draft.* Write the first draft and don't worry about the style or the words – you can sort that out later.
- *Edit the draft and write the final draft.* Check for errors, and make sure that there is a logical flow through the work for your reader to follow.

Preparation

If you have written your presentation in full, then you need to reduce it down to headings and key phrases – very few people can read a presentation effectively without it sounding stilted and dull. You need to make a rough version of the visual aids, handouts and exercises you are going to use. Do a rough walk through and ask yourself whether the visuals are adequate, the sequence works, the balance is correct, does it achieve your purpose? Amend as needed and finalise the visuals and handouts. Have a dress rehearsal in front of a safe audience if possible. The better prepared you are the less "butterflies" you will have.

You would be very unusual if you did not feel nervous before speaking to a large audience. Even famous actors are nervous before the play begins. You will feel less nervous if you are well prepared and concentrate on what you have to say rather than who is in the audience or what you look like.

Make sure you know the facilities available, and that your presentation media will work! Give yourself time before the talk to feel comfortable with the room and the equipment. Check out the lighting, heating etc – you want your audience to see the visuals and not fall asleep in a hot room.

The Organisational Dimension

Giving your talk

Remember that the idea is to communicate to the audience and not to show off!!
Make a good impression – look the audience in the eye and smile, try to establish contact with them. Have a few sentences prepared to get you going, once you have started, it will be easy to keep going. Do not open with clichés, try and say something original and interesting. Maintain contact with the audience, talk to them and not the visuals or your notes. Speak naturally, do not read your notes – they should be a support and not a crutch. Try to imagine you are talking to friends rather than an unknown audience. Vary your pace, tone and sound enthusiastic. If you aren't interested then why should your audience be interested? Appear relaxed and confident, do not fidget or move about too much. If you have trouble with this then try using the lectern or table to anchor yourself. Do not apologise for your lack of knowledge or your shortcomings, you do not want to undermine the audience's confidence in you. Be careful when using humour – do not force it and do not use humour at the audience's expense. Concentrate on communicating, if they have not understood, then it is your fault – watch for signs of boredom, puzzlement, distraction and respond to them – if you see yawns, glances at watches then try and bring them back by re-capping. To help keep the audience awake, think about building in exercises for them to do as you go through the talk. Just as you gained the interest of the audience at the beginning you need a clean finish and then offer the chance to ask questions.

Visual Aids

Visual aids can greatly assist you in communicating. They should be simple and easy to understand. You should give the audience time to read and absorb the information. You can draw attention to important points.

Flip charts - can be quickly improvised or prepared in advance and can be added to during the talk, they also form a record. Keep the lettering bold and simple - however, they can be difficult to see for a large group.
Whiteboards/Chalkboards - useful, but a bit 'down-market' and rather messy. It is difficult to prepare these in advance but they are good for spontaneous use with small groups. You should practice writing on them beforehand to ensure that your writing is readable. Unfortunately, information added during the talk is not retained unless somebody copies it all down.

The Organisational Dimension

Magnetic boards – these must be prepared in advance and are useful if you want to move items about.

Overhead projectors – very versatile, and easily prepared in advance - these now tend to be replaced by the electronic projector. They are portable and can be used spontaneously. However, they can break down and it is useful to have a spare bulb ready.

Slide projectors – very lengthy preparations needed and the lighting in the room needs to be reduced.

Film /Video – can be constraining and expensive. If it is not done professionally then the quality of the acting can undermine the message you are trying to get across.

Electronic projection – Slides can be prepared using a programme such as PowerPoint from Microsoft. These can then be presented from a laptop computer using an electronic projector. Using the laptop also means that you can add in video clips and animation to the presentation. This type of presentation is easy to do, and you can add notes to the bottom of the slides and produce handouts for the talk.

Real Objects - Examples of what you are talking about can be very effective in capturing attention; keep them hidden until they are required.

Nothing can take the place of thorough and sound preparation, and most importantly in speaking – don't rush; you may know what you are going to say but your audience doesn't and they will need time to understand.

The Organisational Dimension

Group Communication

Communication is not just a one-to-one activity, increasingly a team carries out work and this requires communication within the team or group. As business becomes more complex it is unlikely that one person will have all the skills needed to solve a problem, thus there is a group meeting where people with different skills can work at solving the problem together.

Advantages of Groups

Commitment – if you are part of a group making the decision you are more likely to be committed to the decision.
Increased skill set – the members of the group will all have different skills and experiences. This should lead to a better solution/decision than anyone working on his or her own.

The tasks that are particularly suited to groups are:
- when creativity is needed
- when memory or recall of information is important
- when the work needs to be divided up amongst people (preferably represented in the group)
- when there is no 'right' answer and consensus of opinion is needed.

People are more willing to take risky or difficult decisions in a group – the responsibility is shared.

Groups can increase the creativity and ideas available to solve the problem through a variety of techniques; the most common is Brainstorming

The Organisational Dimension

Introduction to Brainstorming

The purpose of brainstorming is to generate as many ideas as possible that come from many different perspectives. The concept is that teams tend to generate more ideas than individuals. As individuals we may run out of ideas quickly, brainstorming in teams is an effective way of obtaining more new ideas. One person's idea may trigger ideas that others would not have thought of by themselves. It is in this way that the team can build on each other's ideas and so trigger individual imagination. The technique is also useful for team building and cohesion. There are many ways in which brainstorming can be carried out. The following guidelines have been created to help ensure a successful brainstorming session.

Guidelines

The team should be sitting in a room away from distraction. Identify the theme or problem that the team wishes to discuss. Sometimes it helps to brainstorm something silly before attempting to brainstorm the chosen theme e.g. *how many uses for a brick?* This can make the team more relaxed. To get the best out of brainstorming there are some simple rules that have been found to work.

Rule 1 Encourage everyone to participate. One way is by taking it in turns to suggest one idea at a time. If an individual cannot think of anything, say, "pass."

Rule 2 There are no silly or bad ideas. Team members should not put each other down by making them feel stupid. Encourage everyone to say whatever comes into his or her head.

Rule 3 Criticism or judgement is not allowed. Team members should not criticise the ideas of others. The idea is to be open minded and constructive.

Rule 4 Discussion of the ideas should not take place until after the brainstorming has finished. Accept everything without comment - it could trigger off new ideas.

Rule 5 Exaggeration and enthusiasm are helpful. There is no such thing as a crazy idea. Very often so-called crazy ideas lead to new ways of thinking and imaginative solutions.

The Organisational Dimension

Rule 6   Look for possible combinations of ideas. In this way the team may arrive at new ideas.

Rule 7   If you run out of ideas try using the six key words - What, When, Where, Why, Who and How.

Rule 8   Build on other people's ideas where possible.

Rule 9   Record all the ideas.

There are different types of brainstorming and some are listed below in Table 2.2.

Brain Storming Approaches	
Advantages	**Disadvantages**
Free Style: The team calls out ideas to be written down (usually on white board or flip chart, by the team leader).	
Spontaneous Can be more creative Possible to build on each others' ideas	Strong personalities may dominate the session Can be confusing if there is too much talking at once
Round Robin: Each team member in turn calls out his or her idea to be written down.	
Difficult to dominate the session Discussion tends to be more focused Everyone is encouraged to take part	Difficult to wait one's turn Loss of spontaneity Embarrassing if cannot think of any ideas -puts participants under pressure as there is reluctance to pass Not as easy to build on others' ideas
Notebook Style: Each team member writes their own ideas on pad or sheet of paper, to be collated later by the team leader.	
Ensures anonymity if sensitive topics are to be discussed Can be used with very large groups Not necessary to speak	Not possible to build on ideas of others Some ideas may not be legible, or understandable Difficult to clarify ideas

Table 2.2 Approaches to Brainstorming

The Organisational Dimension

Brainstorming can produce more high quality and original ideas than one person working on their own.

Disadvantages of Groups

There are disadvantages of working in groups.
- Time - Meetings take time. Even an hour meeting attended by eight people is equivalent to one-man day of work. It can also take more time for a group to reach a decision than an individual. Everybody feels that they need to have their say.
- Pressure - A strong character in the group may intimidate people into a decision they do not agree with.
- Too much talk and no action – If you are not careful the discussion will go on and on and a decision are never reached.

These disadvantages can be controlled and minimised if the group has a strong chair.

Group Effectiveness   *Group Building Roles.*

Plant – A person who is imaginative and has unorthodox ways of solving problems, although the solutions may not be practical. If the group has too many 'plants' then there will be conflicts.

Resource Investigator – An enthusiastic and communicative person who is good at exploring opportunities but can become easily bored.

Co-ordinator – An excellent chairperson, who is confident, clarifies goals and promotes decision-making.

Shaper – A dynamic extrovert who challenges the issues and finds solutions, but can be impatient.

Monitor-Evaluator – A person with good judgement who sees all the options and can think strategically. They are not necessarily imaginative or motivational.

Team worker – Supportive and accommodating, these people help smooth over conflicts and build on others' ideas. They can be indecisive.

Implementer – A reliable and efficient person who can turn ideas into actions. However, they can be resistant to new or unusual ideas.

Completer-Finisher – A person who is conscientious, can spot problems and omissions and importantly finishes things off.

Specialist – A single-minded person who provides specialist or technical skills but usually only contributes on a narrow front.

The Organisational Dimension

Environment

The actual environment can also affect the group's performance. Meetings on neutral ground tend to work best as no one interest group is seen as 'at home'. Sitting around a table is more conducive to equality than other seating arrangements. It is also important to consider the status of the group within the organisation. If it has poor status then nobody will want to belong to it – and decisions may not be taken seriously.

Tasks

Tasks for a group normally fall into 4 main types:
- information sharing
- persuasive (recommending action)
- creative/problem solving
- Decision-making.

Meetings for information sharing, where the objective is to disseminate information, and participants make little contribution, can be larger than meetings where a large amount of interaction is needed and decisions need to be made.

Leadership

The group leader will influence the way the group interacts and meets its goals. There are 3 styles of leadership: Democratic – guiding the group as needed, people in the group will feel satisfied as they will have a chance to contribute to the decision, and there will be a reasonable level of productivity; Autocratic – this group will be dominated by the leader and will be led according to his/her agenda rather than the group's goal; Laissez-faire – the group will become a talking shop and there is little attention given to actually achieving the goals.

The Organisational Dimension

Group Interaction

There are two forms of group interaction
- Communication through the leader
- General communication between members

The method used will depend on the group and the task - each has its place. The first is useful for controlling large meetings, whereas the second is needed for problem solving activities.

Handling Confrontation in Meetings

There are several ways of handling confrontation in meetings.
Compromise – you agree to 'split the difference'.
Confrontation - views are freely exchanged, with the aim of bringing the issues out into the open and working through them.
Smoothing - the differences are smoothed over and ignored for the time being. This approach rarely works in the long run.
Power – the solution is forced upon the group. This will result in upsetting at least one set of people and often more.
Coalition - another way of forcing through a solution, again this may cause problems with at least one faction.

Taking Part in a Group Discussion/Meeting

Whatever the subject, taking part in a group discussion involves a balance of speaking and listening skills. However, it is not always easy to get the balance right. Some people:
- Don't say enough
- Say too much
- Don't listen to others

For good communication to take place in a discussion it is important to:
- Know if the subject is routine or non-routine to the speakers and listeners.
- Be sensitive and make allowances for others who may not know much about the subject.
- Always try to make the others feel valued for what they have to say.
- Get to know as much as possible about the subject to help your own contribution.

The Organisational Dimension

Tips for keeping to the point in discussion:
- Before discussion begins it is useful to state and agree the purpose of the discussion or meeting
'*So the reason why we are discussing this proposal is to agree on the funding requirement.*'
- Sum up regularly during the discussion - how far you have got with the purpose.
'*At this stage it looks like we have agreed on this phase of the funding*'
- Avoid "off the point" discussion. This needs to be done gently. A reminder in the form of a question is often a good method.
'*That's an interesting point, but do you feel it's important to the main purpose of our discussion?*'
- In a group that often work together, it is sometimes a good idea to elect one person in rotation to alert the others when the discussion begins to drift.

Helping Others to Contribute to a Discussion

In a discussion, some people do not find it easy to talk. This increases when the members of a group do not know one another. In these circumstances some people feel shy and uneasy. They feel everything they say will be judged critically. They lack confidence and feel what they have to say is of little value.

Helping others to contribute is a skill in its own right. Here are some methods:
- Help each member of the discussion to express their feelings, views or ideas on the subject by inviting them to speak.
'*John how do you feel about this idea, would you like to say something at this stage?*'
- Make sure each member of the discussion feels they have a right to an equal say.
'*Remember, everyone here has a right to an opinion on this subject. Just speak up when you want to speak.*'
- Show an awareness of gender roles and language in discussion and avoid sexist terms.
'*Which would you prefer chairman or chairperson?*'
- Avoid trying to impress others or to dominate the discussion.
- Listen with the same attention to each member of the group.
- Use body language such as nods and smiles to support others as they talk.

The Organisational Dimension

- Give others time to finish expressing themselves, even though they may hesitate and sometimes struggle for the right word.
- Avoid interrupting.

Checking for Understanding

During a discussion it is important to check your understanding of the points that are made. This helps you to follow the line of argument and keep track of ideas that arise. There are a number of strategies for doing this.
- Stopping the discussion in order to express your view of what has been said.
- Asking others to confirm your understanding.
- Asking others to repeat or re-phrase the points they have made.
- Reflecting back on the discussion with another group member to check your understanding of points made.
- Offering a summary of the discussion to a partner or group of your peers.
- Planning in advance for review during the discussion.

Here are some sound-bites that you can associate with checking and confirming understanding in discussion.

'Are you saying......'

'Am I right in thinking what's been said is.......'

'Would this be a fair summary of what's been said so far......'

'It seems to me there are three main points being made here......'

'It would be useful at this stage to reflect on what has been said......'

Making sure you get your point across

Sometimes the points made in a discussion are not understood. This may be because:
- Points were poorly expressed.
- There was too much detail for others to follow and understand.
- The language was too complex.
- For unknown reasons the listeners were unable to follow the discussion.

The Organisational Dimension

Checking for understanding helps to identify the need to communicate the same information again.
When communication breaks down in this way, it is necessary to re-express the points made in a style more readily understood.

Evaluate the value of your own and other people's contributions to a discussion

By:
- Observation – these questions need to be addressed:
  Is the contribution expressed appropriately?
  Are the tone, pitch and pace correct?
  Do listeners understand the contribution/ do they appear interested?
  Does the contribution make sense and is it relevant?
- Recording – video, tape recordings or even written notes made during a discussion can be very useful sources of evidence.
- Discussion - discussion with a small group of colleagues is a useful way of testing your opinions and assessment of your own and other people's contributions. You can also use the video or tape recorded evidence to help analyse the discussion for skills that need to be developed by individual members (with their permission).

Remember: When you are discussing other people's contributions, it is important to avoid destructive comments. It is generally more helpful to highlight the strengths and to talk of skills for development, rather than faults and weaknesses.

Agreement about the outcome of a discussion

At the end of discussion it is necessary to agree and note the outcome. Sometimes this can be the chairperson's job. At other times the group may decide to appoint a secretary to list the main points as they arise and read them back for agreement at the end. This helps:
- Remind participants of key issues agreed.
- Indicate what was covered and what has still to be covered in discussion.
- Helps to set future targets and agendas for further discussions.

The Organisational Dimension

Tips for Working in groups

- Decide who is going to lead the group
- Decide who is going to make notes
- Each group member should make sure everyone takes part in speaking, listening and doing
- Express your own ideas, comments, examples, etc
- Allow others to have their say
- Support or question the contributions of others
- Discourage anyone who does not take it seriously.

Section 3

The Nature and Context of Project Management

The Nature and Context of Project Management

The Nature and Context of Project Management

Project Definition

There are many definitions of 'project', however, the International Standards Organisation (ISO) defines a project as:

"A unique process consisting of a set of co-ordinated and controlled activities, with start and finish dates, undertaken to deliver a product or result conforming to specific requirements, within the constraints of time, cost and resources"

A project is a "change engine"; at the end of a project something new exists that did not exist before.

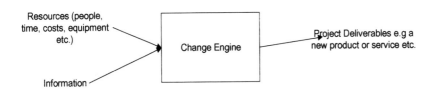

Figure 3.1 The Change Engine of a Project

There is a distinct difference between a project and ordinary work. Most ordinary work (operations) is process orientated and repetitive, whereas a project has a beginning, an end and creates a unique product or service. BS 6079-1:2000 "Project Management", identifies the following as project attributes:

- They are non-repetitive and tend to have significant unique features likely to be novel to management.
- They carry risk and uncertainty.
- They should be approved in return for undertakings to deliver specified (minimum) quantified results within pre-determined quality and safety/health parameters.
- The authorisation should leave no doubt what results will need to be delivered with firm start and finishing dates, within clearly specified cost and resource constraints.
- They are usually in the hands of a temporary team and may be subject to change as the work progresses

The Nature and Context of Project Management

- In a long duration project, events inside and outside the enterprise may affect the outcome.

For a project, once the objectives have been reached the project ends; whereas in operational work, once the objectives have been reached then a new set of objectives are established and the work continues. Figure 3.1 could be applied to both project and operational work – but as we have seen project work has a finite end. Projects tend to be associated with revolutionary change, whereas operational management could be considered more as evolutionary change – continuous improvement. There is no fixed end point; it goes on and on. To illustrate this some examples of project and operational work are shown in Table 3.1.

Project Work	Operational Work
Developing a new product or service	Assembly line production
Constructing a building	Maintaining a building
Opening a new sales office	Responding to a sales enquiry
Writing and publishing a book	Replying to office correspondence
Moving house	Housework
Obtaining ISO9001: 2000 Accreditation	Maintaining a Quality Management System

Table 3.1 Examples of project work and operational work

For instance, answering today's correspondence is operational work. The objective today is to write the letters, but after doing so a new objective is set, that of answering tomorrow's correspondence. Thus operational work is on going and it is to a large extent repetitive. However, writing a book is a project. The objective is to deliver the book to the publishers; once this is completed the job is finished. You may wish to write another book, but that will be another project.

Projects are usually judged successful if they are delivered on time, on budget and of the right quality. This is the standard project triangle, but the project should also make sure the customer (external or internal) is satisfied, this means that it should deliver a product that meets the customer's requirements. This makes a pyramid that is known as the 'Universal Project Pyramid. It is managing the interaction of these elements that is fundamental to *project management*.

The Nature and Context of Project Management

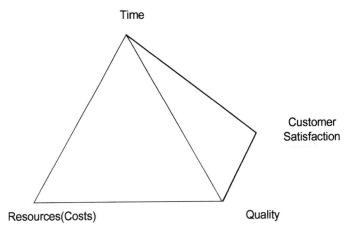

Figure 3.2 The Universal Project Pyramid

Project Management is the process of using systems and techniques together with resources to complete a project to meet a set of objectives. These objectives are based on the scope (customer requirements), time, cost (resources) and quality.

Good project management is also an efficient and effective way of managing change in an organisation. The project management cycle is recognisable as the PLAN-DO-CHECK-ACT cycle from ISO Standards; in project management terms it is seen as PLAN-ORGANISE(EXECUTE)-MONITOR and CONTROL. And so, as well as delivering a project on budget, on time and within agreed specifications, it can also be used as a method of management that allows an organisation to:

- Save money and focus resources on the most important objectives. Project Management ensures identification of the deliverables and that an identified person – the project manager focuses on delivering them.
- Gain consensus and commitment from people involved. The fact that clear objectives have to be identified means that everyone involved in the project has seen and agreed on the deliverables and works towards achieving them.
- Ensure that at an early stage of the project issues such as safety and quality are designed in. Projects are planned, they do not just happen and so safety and quality issues can be identified and planned from the beginning.
- Provide a greater range of experience for staff working on the project. Working on a project can open up different aspects of the business to staff and thus make them more valuable to the organisation.

The Nature and Context of Project Management

- Control a range of initiatives within a business. When business initiatives are managed as projects they are easier to control.

Programme Management A group of projects may be managed together in a co-ordinated programme to obtain benefits not available from managing them individually. All the projects should have some link between them and support each other. Most programmes will also include elements of operational work.

Project Stakeholders These are organisations and people who are either directly involved in the project or have a vested interest in the success of the project. These can include not only the project team but also the investors, directors, clients (if they are the final customer) etc. Major changes in the project will need the support of the stakeholders and they should be kept informed throughout the project.

The Project Environment

The organisation structure is obviously a key factor in the environment within which the project has to function, and it will be discussed later.

Change Environment

The general environment of a project is that of change and this can be a threatening environment for some people. Managers used to stable operational environments may find the rapidly moving project environment tough and stressful to deal with. Even change for good reasons can have a negative effect on people and resentment of change may build up within the project team. This will have to be handled with tact and understanding by the project manager.

Strategic Environment

Projects need to fit into the overall organisation's environment. There should be a recognised business case for the project and a fit within the organisation's strategy. Projects that start on a hunch without contributing real benefits to the business are likely to fail, and if not will have numerous changes to scope that will lead to overruns and dissatisfaction.

The Nature and Context of Project Management

Quality Environment

The senior managers of the organisation are responsible for creating the right environment for quality, both in the project management process and in the final product. This can be achieved through:

- Using data and factual information to make decisions
- Training and developing personnel such that everyone understands their role in achieving quality
- Using an organisational structure that aids project management and helps the project to achieve its objectives
- Developing mutually beneficial supplier relationships so that cost is not the only factor used to choose suppliers and contractors.
- Providing the right tools and techniques for the job
- Delegating a level of authority to the project manager to allow him/her to carry out his responsibilities
- Allowing time at the beginning of the project to understand the scope and develop the project plan. Understanding that time spent here will be more than made up during the project.

You may recognise some of these as similar to the eight principles of Quality Management that the ISO9001: 2000 Standard is based upon:

- Customer focused organisation
- Leadership
- Involvement of people
- Process approach
- System approach to management
- Continual improvement
- Factual approach to decision-making
- Mutual beneficial supplier relationship

Cultural Themes of mar[...]

The Nature and Context of Project Management

Organisational Culture

Organisational culture can have an impact on the project. For example, if the organisation is very conservative, then the project team may not be able to take the risks it feels are appropriate for the project. In a formal organisation, a very relaxed and hands on style of management may cause the team to feel uncomfortable. A project culture is different from an operational culture, the former being more flexible, effective and goal orientated, whilst the latter has stability, efficiency and fixed roles.

The project will also have to follow the organisation's own protocols e.g. purchase order procedures, time keeping, report formats, standard documentation formats etc. Any change from the norms required by the organisation, must be agreed and authorised at the start of the project. For instance, if the staff costs charged to the project have to include on-costs such as, a share of the overheads then it is no good leaving overheads out of the project budget, unless this has been agreed with the finance department prior to the start of the project.

Standards and Regulations

There are two main areas outside the organisation that often affect projects.

Standards and Regulations are differentiated by ISO in the following way:
- A 'standard' is a "document approved by a recognised body, that provides for common and repeated use, rules, guidelines or characteristics for products, processes or services with which compliance is not mandatory".

- A 'regulation' is a "document, which lays down product, process, or service characteristics including the applicable administrative provisions, with which compliance is mandatory".

The project has to follow any standards or regulations that are relevant and reflect any relevant changes in them. If the organisation has accreditation to ISO9001 for its quality management system, then the project must follow processes that fit within the standard's requirements. The same goes for other management standards such as ISO14001 (Environment) and BS7799 (Security). It must also obey any regulations in force that are applicable, such as Health and Safety at Work, Building Regulations etc.

The Nature and Context of Project Management

Many industries also have 'dedicated agencies' to deal with. For example, the pharmaceutical industry in the USA must deal with the Food and Drug Administration (FDA). These agencies usually have to be consulted before undertaking any new projects. In some cases these industries have developed their own standards, based on ISO9001, but taking them further and requiring even greater control e.g. AS9000 for the aerospace industry.

Cultural Influences

Projects must operate within the cultural norms that they find themselves. This includes taking account of economic, demographic, political, ethnic, ethical, religious, educational and other areas of belief, practice and attitudes that affect the way organisations and people interact. For instance, at the end of the week, a wind up with the project team over a beer would be inappropriate in some countries. The cultural norms acceptable for things such as meetings are different through the world; some countries will expect a slower pace and more introductory protocols than others. Problems can be created if you rush ahead assuming that all cultures expect the same behaviour. Background study of the cultural norms of the country or people you are working with may help things go more smoothly.

Projects and Company Organisation Structure

The structure and size of the organisation will inevitably affect the way projects are managed within the organisation. There are 3 generic types of organisational structure.

- Functional
- Project
- Matrix

In fact these structures may be considered a continuum with the functional structure at one end, the project structure at the other, and with the matrix structure somewhere in between.

The Nature and Context of Project Management

Functional Organisation

This is the traditional form of organisation with separate functional departments for sales and marketing, production, development etc. There is usually no separate project or project management function. In this type of organisation people maybe assigned from a permanent functional department to serve the requirements of a temporary project, often on an as and when basis. This does have the benefit of calling on specialist resources from the functional departments and expertise available for the project is often high.

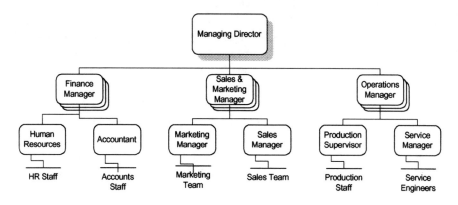

Figure 3.3 Example Functional Organisation Structure

Rather than assigning people from different functional departments to the project, the project may be small enough to be contained within one functional group. The advantages of this approach are the simple reporting structure and clear lines of authority. Further, when the project staff are within one group, the team members are already familiar with each other's strengths and weaknesses and there is no interdepartmental conflict.

The Nature and Context of Project Management

However, there can be disadvantages for a project that is kept within a functional group:

- Isolation of the project from other parts of the organisation - for example, a project to introduce a new piece of production equipment that is given to the Production Department could suffer, because without input from the Service Department the new equipment may not be able to deal efficiently with repairs or returns.
- Limited skills - not all the required skills may be available in the group.
- Lack of priority – the functional work will still have to be carried out and may conflict with the project work.

When the project grows and no 'functional group' owns the project, for example, a project to develop a new product will have implications for Marketing and Sales, Development, Production and Service, then other problems can occur. In this case the Project Manager may report directly to the Managing Director and require people to be assigned to him for particular tasks, and he should be aware that:

- Functional specialists can favour their own specialisms, rather than the objectives of a project.
- Functional heads may be unwilling to release staff for a project; it may have a negative impact on their operations. (Letting production staff attend a development meeting may decrease productivity.)
- Staff released for a project by functional heads may be the least able and this may have a negative impact on project performance.
- Depending on the accounting arrangements functional managers may be able to charge staff time to projects. This could lead to over-charging on the project to the benefit of the functional groups.
- Absence of project-orientated systems (e.g. finance) makes the project management more difficult as costs may be harder to track.
- A project split over the departments may suffer because of conflicting resource requirements that need to be balanced at a senior level. This can mean an overstretched Chief Executive.

The Nature and Context of Project Management

Project based Organisation

The project form of an organisation is where people are allocated on a full-time basis to work exclusively on a project. Each team is self-contained and under the direction of a single project manager. The strength of the structure comes from the singleness of purpose and unity of command.

There are problems if a temporary structure is designed for a sole project. It can disturb the on-going organisation, some project resources might duplicate those in permanent departments, and also anxiety and insecurity can arise in team members because of the short duration of the project. Clashes can occur between long-term objectives of permanent departments striving for economic technical excellence and the short-term objective of a temporary project striving to satisfy targets of time, budget, quality and safety.

A permanent project structure is less common and is usually found in two types of organisation.

- Organisations where their business is performing projects for others e.g. architects, quantity surveyors, construction contractors.
- Organisations who have decided to use management by projects as their management approach. They treat many on-going operations as projects so that project management techniques can be used to control them.

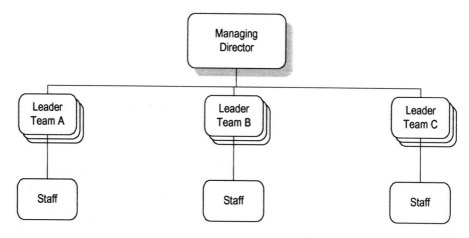

Figure 3.4 Project Organisation Structure

The Nature and Context of Project Management

In this type of organisation the benefits are:

- Project authority is clear – no conflict with a functional role
- Simple project communications – all team members are in one team
- Strong project focus and clear priorities – fewer distractions
- The administration system is set up to support project needs e.g. finance controls are project based.

Typically the project team is multidisciplinary and moves from one project to the next. The disadvantages of this style of organisation are:

- The team may be working on more than one project at once and so there will still be conflicts, only in this case between projects.
- Over-resourcing – if each team has its own skill set, then there may be duplication of specialist skills that are only required for small elements of each project. This will increase the costs of the individual projects.
- Staff uncertainties - at the end of a project the staff may be concerned that they will be made redundant if there are no new projects. This may mean they spin out a project to last as long as possible.
- Project teams may compete with each other. This can be positive if handled well, but can lead to unproductive protectionism of skills or ideas. One team may have already solved a problem but will not share their solution with another team.

Matrix Organisation

In most organisations there is a mix between a functional and a project organisation. People come from various departments to form a multi-disciplinary project team. They are in effect responsible to two managers – the functional manager and the project manager. This hybrid structure attempts to maximise the strength and minimise the weakness of the other two types of structure. It uses the vertical management of functional structure with the horizontal management of the project structure. The strength of the structure comes from the balance of long-term functional objectives and short-term objectives of the project. This means operating in a structured way across functional boundaries to meet the objectives of the project. The main weakness is the fact the people may have two managers, a functional manager and the project manager. Senior management must define roles, authorities and responsibilities to avoid any ambiguity for the project and the functional manager. Typically, the project manager concentrates on what is to be done and when (timing and budget -

The Nature and Context of Project Management

effectiveness), whilst the functional manager concentrates on who does it and how it is done (methods and quality - efficiency). The project manager must set realistic plans and programmes whilst the functional manager must be psychologically committed to the assigned work packages.

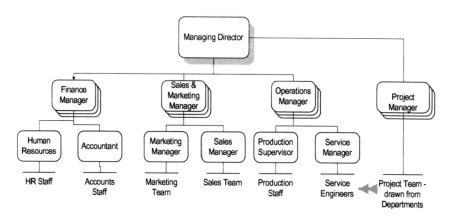

Figure 3.5 Example Matrix Structure

There are a variety of ways a matrix organisation can operate.

Balanced Matrix

The project manager shares responsibility with the functional managers; he/she is responsible for time and cost whilst the functional manager is responsible for scope and quality. This can be a difficult balancing act and its success is very dependent on the relevant strengths of the managers involved.

Co-ordinated (weak) matrix

A project controller is appointed with responsibility for co-ordinating tasks, but has a limited authority over the resources needed to accomplish the tasks. This leaves the project co-ordinator in an unenviable position with essentially no resource of their own and continual negotiation to gain resource.

The Nature and Context of Project Management

Secondment (strong) matrix

The project manager has primary responsibility for tasks and the functional managers assign people as required. The project manager now has more effective control with resources seconded to him.

The advantages of a matrix organisation are:

- Staff flexibility and opportunities – staff can be assigned from departments, as they are needed. People from departments are exposed to other skills and interests and the new experiences lead to more effective employees.
- Rapid response to market. A matrix organisation can adapt more quickly to changing technologies and market. The multi-disciplined team can be formed with defined responsibility to respond to a change. The mix of skills and experiences can lead to a quicker and more effective response. The marketing people may be enlightened by the experiences of the service staff, who visit the clients "on the ground".
- It combines the strengths of both the functional organisation and the project organisation.

The disadvantages of matrix structures are:

- Conflicts between line and project duties and priorities. People will have several managers and several roles within a company.
- Team members may like the project role more than their functional role and may resist returning to their operational job. This can delay project close as members drag their feet.

In most cases the project manager is stuck with whatever organisational structure is in place. It is unlikely that the organisation will be changed for the benefit of a project. Also any such transition is likely to cause great upheaval and take a considerable time. To change from a functional organisation to a matrix organisation, has been shown to take 3 – 5 years for a large organisation.

The Nature and Context of Project Management

Project Life Cycle

Every project has a life cycle that takes it from birth "initiation" to death "project close". Different industries use different terminologies to describe these phases and may have more or less of them. However, a generic lifecycle could have the following phases:

Phase 1 Proposal - Conception
- Project definition
- Scope and business objectives

Phase 2 Feasibility
- Functional design
- Initial estimates
- Go/no go decision

Phase 3 Design and Appraisal - Implementation
- System design
- Planning and resourcing
- Estimates
- Construction
- Installation
- Monitor and Control

Phase 4 Execution – Operation
- Launch
- Education and communication
- Monitor progress
- Maintaining the project

Phase 5 Finalisation and Close down - Termination
- Achievement of benefits
- Disbanding and rewarding the team
- Audit and review
- Historical records

The interface between each phase is often called a milestone and provides a suitable point for review. The resources used at each phase will differ; but most lifecycles share a common staffing and cost pattern. Slow at the beginning, higher towards the middle and dropping quickly as the project is concluded. Figure 3.6 shows how most projects use resources over time.

The Nature and Context of Project Management

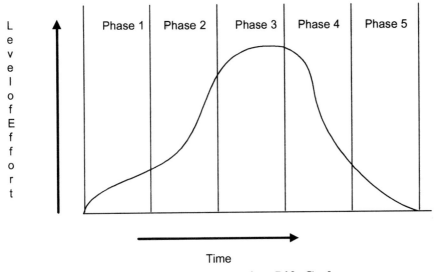

Figure 3.6 An Example of a Generic Project Life Cycle

Within the project phases various project management processes take place. A process is "a series of actions that bring about a result". Confusingly these processes can have similar names to the project phases. In the case of a project, there are five basic management processes: Initiating, Planning, Executing, Controlling and Closing. These will be discussed in more detail later. A key difference between a process and a phase is that the phases in a life cycle are linear (they happen one after the other), whereas the project management processes recur through the project – they can occur in every phase. The processes can also overlap within a phase as shown in Figure 3.7.

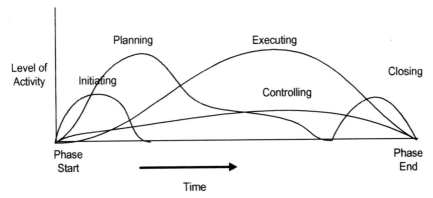

Figure 3.7 Overlap of Processes in a Phase

The Nature and Context of Project Management

In a major project there will probably be a formal handover between each phase and this may result in the release of the next tranch of the budget. Even in small projects where there is no formal handover, the phases will still be seen. At the end of each phase there is usually one or more deliverables e.g. feasibility study, detailed design, prototype. The deliverables from the preceding phase are usually approved before work can begin on the next phase. If a later phase is started prior to approval of the earlier phase, this is known as fast tracking.

Phases in the Project Life Cycle

1. Proposal (Conception) Phase

Conception is usually the first phase of the project life cycle. It covers the period from the generation of the idea, through to a draft project brief covering development of the scope of the project and the identification of the business objectives for it – how will it meet a user's or sponsor's needs.
Ideas for projects may be generated from customer feedback, advances in technology, competitor actions etc. During this phase everybody involved is encouraged to generate ideas and solutions to satisfy the need, or to solve the particular problem. The project manager may not be in place at this time, although if someone has already been identified it is beneficial to consult him/her.

If the organisation is undertaking the project on behalf of a client, then it is at this stage that the expectations of the client both implicit and explicit must be defined. If the project manager does not understand what the client wants the project to deliver, then he cannot be sure of delivering it. This will lead to a dissatisfied client and usually increases the cost of the project, as changes have to be made to make the deliverables match the requirements. It is worth spending enough time at this stage to get the project scope and definition understood – whether internal or external, because clear understanding here will save time and money later on in the project.

The Nature and Context of Project Management

The starting point for avoiding any confusion over the project deliverables is the setting of clear project objectives. A helpful way to set objectives is to use the SMART Acronym.

Specific – a clear, unambiguous statement of what is required
Measurable – success criteria established, with clearly defined start and end point
Achievable – the objective must be within the capability of the project to deliver
Relevant – they should be relevant to the project
Time Limits Set – start and finish dates, durations

There are four principles that help in setting successful objectives.
- Communication – communicate them within the project team
- Ownership – involve everyone in the discussions – people are more motivated to achieve them if they have contributed to them
- Agreement and understanding - check that all the team understand them
- Individual input – determine an appropriate level of input from members and encourage them to contribute.

At the end of this stage there should be approval from management to proceed to the feasibility stage, together with the commitment of resources. The scope of the project should have been defined, even if it is not clear how will it be achieved – this is investigated in the feasibility phase.

2. Feasibility Phase

No project can deliver the desired benefit if it is impossible to complete. To find out if the project is possible is done in a structured manner by carrying out a feasibility study. The objective is to establish technical and financial feasibility, and where appropriate, commercial feasibility. It should:

- Explore all possible options for implementing the project
- Achieve a clear understanding of the issues involved
- Produce enough information so that the options can be ranked
- Obtain a clear picture of how to proceed

The study must assess the options available and understand what factors may influence the success or failure of these options. Factors to be considered could be:

The Nature and Context of Project Management

Market Conditions
- Is there a market demand for the product?
- What price will the market bear – will it give a return on the investment?
- Is the market volatile?
- What competitors are there?

Supply Considerations
- Cost, quality and availability of capital equipment, raw material, skilled labour.
- Technical options – is it technically possible at the price?

Financial Prospects
- Is the expected return sufficient to finance the debt and provide shareholders with an adequate return?

The processes within the feasibility study are the standard project processes.

Initiate the Study
- Appoint the team (this is the team for the feasibility study, it may or may not be the same as the project team) – there should be a good balance between specialists. If they are all technical then there may be a bias towards a highly technical approach, because they want to use the latest technology. Alternatively, if they are all sales people, they may overlook some key practicalities.
- Examine the scope of the study and understand any constraints involved. Agree, where possible on the timescale and deliverables of the feasibility study.
- Appoint any external advisors if they will be required to supplement the expertise of the team. Where appropriate, obtain certain permissions and consents. For example, it would be wise to check on planning consent before planning to build a new office block.
- Plan the study.
- Set a timetable and budget for the study.

The Nature and Context of Project Management

*Manage the Study (*Planning and Execution*)*
- Establish roles and responsibilities of those taking part in the study.
- Communicate within the team to ensure everybody knows what is going on and ensure all information has been made available to everyone.
- The information may cover initial estimates of the cost of the project, both in financial terms and non-financial resources, including an assessment of probable income generation and operational costs such as production, distribution and marketing.
- Deliverables may include the business case as well as the technical feasibility.
- A basic risk analysis may be undertaken. The range of solutions may be investigated in terms of risk, as well as technical feasibility and cost.
- Consideration of technical feasibility, economic feasibility and operational feasibility. Are the concepts practical, can it be developed into a useful working product or service? What is the market demand for the product or service? Is there any price sensitivity?

*Control the Study (*Control*)*
- The manager must ensure that milestones are reached, costs controlled and the deliverable – the feasibility report delivered.

*Closure (*Closing*)*
- Delivery of the feasibility report to the overall Project Team and senior management. The report should contain:
    - Technical review of the possible solutions
    - Evaluation of the preferred solution together with supporting evidence for this preference
    - Identification of any risk areas or possible difficulties together with a view of their probability
    - Plans on how to take the project forward
    - Estimates of the likely resource requirements such as money, time, skill base, plant etc
    - Any other issues e.g. product future, close down costs.
- The senior management take the go/no go decision and the resources for the next stage of the project are released.

The Nature and Context of Project Management

Failure to identify any problems with the project at this stage can cause extensive problems in later stages. It is much easier to correct an outline specification than implement modifications to a product in the field. Although this stage is often considered a "waste of time" and people are eager to start "doing" the project, the importance of the stage should not be overlooked. The stage may even decide that the project is not worth doing!

3. Implementation Phase

This is usually the largest phase of the project and encompasses all the activities associated with actually doing the main tasks of the project. This could include; a more detailed development of the chosen solution with more accurate assessments of cost and time, the design and development of the project or service, the purchasing of any required parts or plant needed for manufacture, the manufacturing, construction or assembly of the product along with any commissioning and acceptance testing.

Work Packages will be given out to people on the project team. These packages should have clear deliverables and all the relevant information should be available for doing the work. The project leader should check that recipients have the resources available to do the work and that they are given a clear go-ahead to proceed. The recipient of the work must be committed to carrying it out and should not feel that it has just been dumped on them; they must believe that the work can be achieved within any constraints, if not, then it will be very de-motivating.

During this phase the project manager must control the project and keep track of the resources being used. There should be reports of costs and resources used to date and estimates of the total expected costs by the end of the project.

Within this phase there are some key handover points, e.g. from development into production, from production into final commissioning. These points are just as important when a service is being developed as when a physical product is being manufactured. These stages may not all be sequential; this is especially the case if items for manufacture or plant have a long delivery. The project manager will need to handle this with care. Ordering parts too early, before the design has been finalised could be a problem if the part specification changes. Alternatively, ordering them too late could cause a mid-project delay, where no progress can be made.

The Nature and Context of Project Management

The deliverable at the end of this phase is the product or service, having met the product requirements, being handed over to the customer for commissioning. It may involve a series of acceptance procedures, and the responsibility for the project may transfer from the Project Manager to the Client or Service Organisation who is responsible for installation.

4. Operational Phase

This is usually the actual use of the product or service. The main activities apart from using the product or service are:
Marketing and selling the product
Servicing the product
Monitoring the product
Identifying any modification or further developments required

Recognising that the definition of a project is that it has a defined end, then as soon as the marketing, selling, servicing and monitoring of the product become established operational processes, this phase can come to an end. The reason for including it in an overall project is to make sure that the product does actually meet the customer requirements and that any loose ends have been closed.

5. Termination Phase

It is during this phase that the project team is disbanded. The return of seconded staff should be handled carefully, otherwise there may be a reluctance to leave the project and this will increase the staffing costs unnecessarily. Some projects may have a major termination activity e.g. decommission of plant or decontamination of a laboratory. For others it may just be the tidying up of loose ends of documentation and archiving. It is important to spend time closing down the project in an orderly fashion and one of the key things to do in this phase is a project 'wash up'. This is an opportunity to review the project, identify areas for improvement, ideas for future projects etc. This review and documentation can provide important information for future projects, help build up the 'body of knowledge' within the company and reduce the risks on future projects.

The Nature and Context of Project Management

Work breakdown structures (WBS)

A Work Breakdown Structure (WBS) is a product oriented "family tree" of project components. It defines and organises the scope of the project. It is a technique for breaking down the project into smaller physical parts so they can be handled more effectively. Although the commonest form of WBS is product based; a project can also be broken down by activities or cost elements. The project is broken into manageable tasks that can be assigned, scheduled, tracked and organised. Each item in the structure can then be allocated a cost, time, quality and safety regime. The benefits for using a WBS are that it provides better control of the project and allows work to be delegated in packages.

A WBS does not attempt to indicate the sequence in which work will be done. It only identifies what must be done. By selecting the items at any level in the WBS diagram, a logic diagram (network) for the project at this specific level of detail can be constructed. When the network diagram is processed a GANTT chart (schedule) can be derived. (Network diagrams are covered later). Through the WBS diagram the project becomes a hierarchical structure of tasks, a task in the middle being a child of a task above and a parent of a task below. Most project plans will have three or four levels of WBS.

The complete project is the single top-level task of the WBS. The hierarchy of tasks allows task information to be summarised at different levels of detail. If a project is too "shallow" there is a risk that tasks are not defined in enough detail. If it is too "deep" then there will be too much detail. The smallest unit in the WBS should be the smallest unit of work to be tracked – the task level. It is only the task level (work package) that is assigned a time estimate and a cost. If there are too many elements the project manager will be swamped by too much reporting and unable to see the "woods for the trees". Everything else in the WBS is simply an organisational tool for summarising how the tasks combine to complete the components of the project. A useful test for a task is to see if it contributes to the output of the parent task – if it does then it is a valid task, if not, then you should question whether it should be included. Another way to judge the lowest-level task to be used in an WBS is to use a budget or time cut off, e.g. the lowest level task should be at least 1 day in time or 0.5% of budget. On projects of a year's duration, then activities of 2 weeks may be considered the lowest appropriate level for planning and control. There should be a single owner for each task, although one person may have more than one task. They are

The Nature and Context of Project Management

accountable to the project leader for their tasks. The owner may not always be a member of the project team e.g. supplier, manager with required resources for the task. Tasks can be combined to become subprojects or milestones. Unless each task has an owner the project manager will find it difficult to manage the project.

Building a task list for a large project will take time, but this list allows the overall amount of work to be assessed and sequenced in a logical fashion. The tasks should account for the production of every deliverable that was approved for the project.

Instead of defining all the tasks first and then working out the deliverables, a milestone plan can be produced first. This plan can then provide a framework for the project. The tasks are fitted into the framework. A milestone plan is also a way of developing co-operation and commitment to the project as it shows what has to be achieved at each stage.

Task identification begins with defining the tasks in the statement of requirements and then expanding to the necessary level of detail. Each task should have a means to measure the performance of the task owner; so short tasks or long tasks with regular deliverables can be used as a basis of performance measurement. Each task will be allocated a time period and a cost for completion. A task can also be defined as critical or non-critical; if a critical activity is embedded within a task it may need breaking out into a separate task. Similarly, the degree of risk associated with the task can be identified, again as with a critical activity, if a high-risk activity sits within a task it may need breaking out into a separate task.

Tasks may be common to many projects and some organisations will have standard task units, often with the time to complete the task already established. Standardised task units should be reviewed regularly by the organisation, as technology, for example, can change the time taken for the task. Care should also be taken to understand what the standard task unit means – is it exactly the same as the work that is being planned?

Once a list of tasks has been established then each task should have its own statement of work. (Statement of Work is also often used as a description of work for the entire project, and so take care not to confuse them). For parent tasks this may just be a summary of the work of the child tasks.

The Nature and Context of Project Management

The statement of work contains, for instance:

- Task number or reference (to uniquely identify it from other tasks)
- Description of the work, with references to any detailed reference documents for the work
- The name of the task owner
- Deliverables, including acceptance criteria
- Timescales for the deliverables
- Schedule of task dependencies and subsidiary tasks. Tasks do not exist in isolation and this task may require others to be completed before it can start and it may well affect the progress of other tasks
- Costs – both in man hours and materials
- Risks
- Performance measurements
- Reporting requirements e.g. performance statement, schedule status, cost status, changes that might affect task deliverables, changes to risk exposure.

Once the project is running the feedback from the task owners will give the project manager the information needed to manage the project. The project manager uses the data from all the tasks to re-run the project plan, the critical task may have changed or tasks may need extra resource to bring them into line. The WBS is likely to change through a project, particularly a large one. Tasks are split up, re-assigned etc and so version control is required. This means that each version should be dated, old versions marked superseded and all team members informed. Everyone needs to be working with the latest version.

The Nature and Context of Project Management

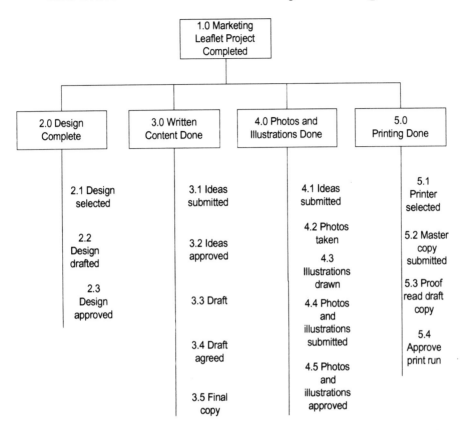

Figure 3.8 A Work breakdown structure for producing a marketing leaflet

The detailed task list and WBS identify the tasks in the project but will only show hierarchical relationships; they do not display the sequencing of the project. Network diagrams are an easier way to identify and plan task sequences. (See Networking)

The Nature and Context of Project Management

Control and Review of Projects

One of the main jobs of the project manager is to control the project on a day-to-day basis. Project control is usually carried out by comparing the current status with the project plan. To control the project successfully, the project manager should:

- Use the project plan as the guide for co-ordinating the project
- Consistently monitor and update the project plan, tasks etc so that the current state is correctly reflected
- Communicate – use the plan to keep in control of the project and to keep other people involved
- Monitor regularly:
    Status of work versus plan
    Volume of work versus plan
    Quality of work
    Cost and expenditure versus plan
    Attitudes of people – staff and customers
    Team spirit
- Act on significant variances, the earlier the better, and then:
    Communicate project status and changes to other team members
    Keep management and customers informed
    Provide justification for making project adjustments
    Document changes to plans

There are two forms of control to be considered; *Proactive control* (authorising work packages, review meetings etc.) and *Reactive control* (taking corrective actions – putting the project back on course). Clear project documentation and effective change control is needed for successful control and review of projects.

Project Documentation

Project documentation allows a consistent approach to be developed and ensures that everyone understands what his or her responsibilities are. The requirements for project quality assurance also mean that there must be evidence of reviews and records of any actions and responsibilities resulting from them. This documentation also allows improvement opportunities to be passed onto future projects and provides follow on information for staff joining the project. Usually the project leader will maintain a project file.

The Nature and Context of Project Management

This will include all the plans, budgets, control and review documentation; this could be in either hard copy or stored on a computer.

Electronic Communication

Electronic communication techniques are now playing a greater role in the management of project documentation. Major projects may use an Extranet site to store the project information. This allows all the project documentation to be held on one external website and accessed by all members of the project team. This is particularly useful if the project team comprises members from several organisations e.g. on construction projects it is accessed by architects, quantity surveyors, project managers, construction companies etc. It ensures that everyone can view the latest documentation and know that they are working from the latest version. An extranet is a considerable investment and should not be undertaken without careful thought.

Objectives for using an extranet on a construction project, for example, could be:
Specific e.g. improve communications, reduce the need for hard copy information
Measurable e.g. design time using electronic communication measured against similar projects using hard copy data.
Achievable e.g. everyone on the project must buy into the extranet and commit the required resource
Realistic e.g. speed of communication increased – this may reduce the time for the project
Timeframe e.g. at what stages will the extranet be used.

You need to plan for the extranet and identify the resources needed to operate it. It is also important to review the risks – what happens if the extranet goes down – what sort of response do the service providers offer to rescue this situation. You also need to consider the risks of data loss and the hacking of sensitive information.

The Nature and Context of Project Management

Change Control

Change is inherent in all projects and successful projects are those where changes are well managed and controlled. All changes must be agreed with the project manager and the task owner. The project will change because no project ever goes completely to plan and so variations occur. Some of these variances will be minor but others will require the project manager to seek senior management approval. The point at which the project manager must go to higher authority is the "tolerance point". Senior Management, prior to the start of the project should set the tolerances for the project. These are set for costs and time, and give the project manager his "freedom" to manage within. If there is evidence that the project will go out of the tolerance band, the project manager should not wait until it does so, but raise the problem as soon as possible with the management. The earlier a problem is identified the more chance there is of bringing it back under control. Variations may be the result of a change of mind by the task sponsor (usually the person or organisation providing the finances), changes in resource, environment, government policy etc. The project manager is responsible for controlling the project plan and all changes must be controlled. The key to keeping control of the changes is a change control process as shown in Figure 3.9. The procedure should seek to analyse (identify), assess, prioritise, plan and control.

The Nature and Context of Project Management

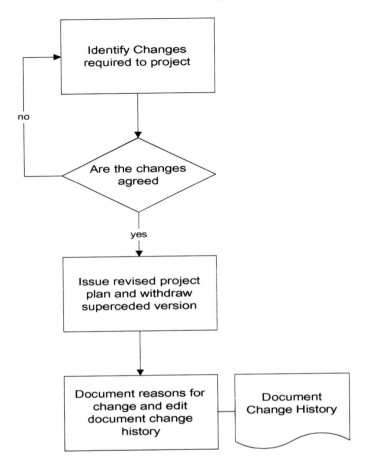

Notes:
1. Check that the revised plan still meets any contractual arrangements
2. Minor changes that are within existing commitments may mean that the plan can be amended without a full re-issue

Figure 3.9 Example Change Control Process

The Nature and Context of Project Management

Reactive Control

The "Reactive control" events will be driven by changes. There are five basic things that could change.

1. Goals and Specifications or Scope – Any changes to the scope of the project should be controlled. It should not be allowed to change without the correct level of authorisation. Changing the scope of a project may or may not require adjustments to cost, time, quality or other project objectives. Scope changes must be fed back through the planning process so that any plans are updated and the relevant people informed.

2. Resources and Materials (including personnel) - The people doing the project could leave, be found to have insufficient skill etc. The materials may be delivered late or of incorrect quality and so on.

3. Cost – Controlling cost means managing the processes required to deliver the project within the approved budget. Cost control requires the project manager to understand which factors will have an impact on costs, know when any of these factors have changed and what effect that has and manage these changes. Cost performance (spend against budget) must be monitored so that any variance from plan can be spotted. If changes have been agreed then the variances must be added to the budget and the affected people informed. As with time, any corrections to costs can have an affect on the time scales and quality of the project. Cost control includes finding out why there have been variances – both positive and negative. Underspends can be just as much of a problem as overspends, it may mean that something has been skipped or mean that a lower grade item has been supplied.

4. Time - Project time management means controlling the processes required to deliver the project on time. Time control is achieved by maintaining the project schedule. The project schedule includes at least the planned start and finish dates for each activity. For time control the project manager needs to understand which factors can create schedule changes, know when any of these factors have occurred and how this has affected the schedule and finally manage the impact of these changes on the schedule. Time control must be integrated with the other control processes – the relationship between time, money and quality means that you are unlikely to be able to change one without having an impact on the others. (The development of the time schedule will be discussed later.) Everybody involved in the project needs to complete a timesheet, if the timesheet method is used to monitor

The Nature and Context of Project Management

time. These should be completed regularly and as accurately as possible. If they are not completed on time then there may be a delay in identifying problems.

5. *Quality* – The other point in the control triangle with money and time is quality. Controlling the quality of the project means ensuring that the project continues to meet the requirements of the customer, complies with any relevant quality standards and any causes of unsatisfactory quality are dealt with. It is important to remember this factor; it is very tempting to bring projects back on budget and schedule by compromising quality. This can mean additional costs later on in the project lifecycle, such as reliability problems. There are two aspects of project quality to consider; product results (the quality of the deliverables) and process results (the cost and schedule performance). (See Project Quality Management).

Any change will affect at least one – and often all five of the above items. The project manager controls the project by responding to these changes, he/she could:

- Re-estimate the project (can things be done better or differently to achieve the same goals?)
- Add more people (this will add to the costs and in some cases 'too many cooks spoil the broth')
- Increase productivity (e.g. by using higher skilled staff who could work more quickly)
- Use consultants/contractors (again this will increase the cost)
- Overtime (more money)
- Crash the schedule (start the next phase before the previous phase has been completed), this may introduce more risk into the project.
- Adjust profit requirements
- Reduce project deliverables – the most likely option as long as the project sponsor agrees.
- Abort the project – this would only be done with agreement from the senior management.

The Nature and Context of Project Management

Proactive Control and Project Review

The key part of the proactive control is 'project review'

Initial Review

Prior to instigation the project will already have come through several review processes to be given the go-ahead to proceed, and to release the funding for the project (internal) or to accept the order from the client (external). In the external case this will mean a contract review giving the organisation's go ahead that they have the resources to deliver the project to the customer's satisfaction. (Table 3.2 is an example checklist for reviewing quotations and orders.) For internal projects this will mean Board or Senior Management review. At this level the reviewers are more interested in the top-level budgets, resources and deliverables – not the operational details of actually running the project.

The Nature and Context of Project Management

Customer (Requirements) Order - Check List							
Customer Number	Order Number		Date				
Customer Name	Customer Address						
Responsibilities for approval shown thus "X"	Sales	Financial & Legal	Technical	Procurement	Production		
Product/Services Defined?	X		X	X			
Installation, Commissioning, Training and Support Defined?			X				
Customer Contractual Requirements Defined?	X	X	X	X			
Unspecified Customer Requirements identified? I.e. Issues which will affect the products or services fitness for purpose but not specified by the customer. E.g. Product or Service Health & Safety.	X		X				
Prices Correct?	X						
Delivery Times Acceptance?			X	X	X		
Customer Financial Health Acceptable?		X					
Supplier's Terms & Conditions accepted by Client?		X					
Customer Terms & Conditions acceptable?		X					
Legal or Regulatory consideration acceptable?			X				
Any special Quality Assurance requirements (e.g. special customer tests)?	X		X				
Signatures and dates							

Table 3.2 General Review Check list Customers enquiries, quotations and orders

The Nature and Context of Project Management

On-going Project Review

Once the project is underway, review meetings may continue to be held with the customer to keep them informed and to ensure that the project is progressing in line with their expectations. However, the most instructive reviews for the project manager are those held with the team to actually find out what is going on and to solve any problems that may have arisen. Reviews will also be held at key points throughout the project, usually at the key milestones and are often accompanied by an acceptance style process e.g. handover from prototype to final design.

Meetings

The project review meetings will be scheduled throughout the project. Unscheduled ones may also be called to deal with difficult situations as they develop. The agenda may differ depending on the stage in the project that has been reached. The example agenda shown in Table 3.3 is for a design review that would be held at the design stage of the project.

Agendas may differ according to the project but all meetings should:
- Start on time
- Use an agenda – including priorities, plans to meet objectives etc.
- Encourage open communication (one person should not dominate)
- Make decisions
- Ensure actions are minuted and agreed
- Finish on time
- Distribute minutes within 2-3 days.

The Nature and Context of Project Management

Design/Project Review Meeting		
Project Name:	Project Number:	Project Manager:
Distribution:		Date:
Items		Remarks
I. **Specification:** A. Mechanical Specification B. Electrical Specification C. Services & Support Specification (Training, Technical etc.) D. Any amendments to specification? E. Will performance still be as defined?		
II. **Target dates:** What is the status of the following (are they still on target)? A. Design B. Purchasing C. Release for production D. Installation & Commissioning		
III. **Design/Project review:** A. Safety factors/requirements (FMEA) B. Drawing; General Arrangements, Detail C. Calculations		
IV. **Status of documentation:** A. Inspection & Test Instructions B. Project & Quality Plan completed C. Installation & Commissioning Instructions D. Operating, service and maintenance manuals		
V. **Approvals:** A. Customer Approval B. Third Party Approval		
VI. **Commercial aspects:** A. Is the project within budget, if not what are proposed actions? B. Is the project within time scale, if not what are proposed actions? C. Invoice & Payment Received		
VII. **Any other business?**		

Table 3.3 Typical Agenda for a Design Review Meeting

The Nature and Context of Project Management

Project Reports

A project manager needs to know what is going on in the project; otherwise he/she will not be able to control it. There are simple forms or reports that are useful for gathering regular feedback information. The review and analysis of data from the project means that the project manager can address problems at an early stage. It may also allow the manager to take advantage of beneficial opportunities. Do not assume that all reviews are about correcting mistakes; they can also look at improving performance.

Reports should be made regularly. The frequency of reporting will depend on: the length of the project, the stage in the project, the risk and consequences of failure and the review level required. There are some standard reports that are useful.

Status Report

Team members should report back on the parts of the WBS that they are responsible for. This report should include:
- Tasks completed since last status report (with dates)
- Tasks in progress and expected dates for completion
- Tasks planned and expected dates for completion
- Budget expenditure; actual costs reported against planned costs and variances
- Issues that need dealing with
- Suggestions for improvement or change
- Outstanding questions
- Earned value (see below)

Earned Value

Earned value measurement is a method of performance reporting and it can be used to calculate schedule and cost variances. When comparing the actual rate of expenditure with the expected rate of expenditure, it is no good assuming that if they are the same then all is well. The money may well have been spent but the work may not be completed. To control costs, you have to look at the work done. The estimated cost of the actual work done is called the earned value. Cost is controlled by comparing the earned value to the actual expenditure and a cost variance is calculated.

The Nature and Context of Project Management

Cost variance = Actual cost of work completed (what you have spent) − earned value (estimate of work done).

% variance = variance/earned value

If the variance is positive, the project is overspent; if it is negative then it is under spent.

In this calculation you usually only look at the activities finished to estimate the value of work done. However, at any point in the project there will also be some work–in–progress and this may also need to be considered. A graph can be plotted of earned value and actual cost of work completed against time. This can provide a visual view of under or over spends.

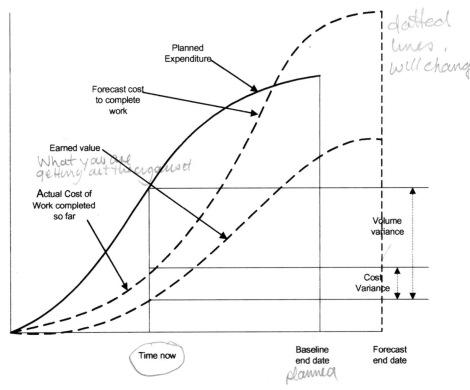

Figure 3. 8 Plotting time and cost variances

The Nature and Context of Project Management

The project manager has three basic control actions depending on the results shown on the graph.
- *No or negligible variance*: continue – no change needed
- *Significant but recoverable:* plan recovery
- *Large*: revise estimates and raise with senior management.

The project leader must also check on the status reports provided by the task owners. Are they a correct view of what is being done? The task owner may be under/over estimating time to completion and think he can make up time later. Walk and talk is a vital part of the monitoring process.

Highlight Report

This type of report is often produced monthly and is aimed at senior management. It contains information about activities completed, plans for the next period, potential problems and their planned solutions. It is presented as an overview and should not take more than a page of A4 paper.

Exception Report

This report may be produced when tolerances might be exceeded – to describe a forecast deviation. It would include the forecast deviation and options for the way forward, including the reasons for the recommended option. It may be presented as a formal report to the senior management team, particularly if the exception will have severe implications for the project deliverables.

Financial Reports

The finance department may be able to provide the 'spend to date', commitment to date, and hours worked for the project. However, this bare information must be treated carefully. The hours and spend may indicate that the project is 50% completed, BUT it doesn't tell you whether the project **is** 50% completed. Thus the need to look at earned value analysis.

The project manager must release the funds as needed by the task owners to carry out the tasks. Small overspends may be covered within the project contingency (reserve) but large overspends will need senior management involvement, since either additional funds will have to be allocated or the project objectives will have to be downsized. Change in the pattern of spend is also important as this may result in unacceptable cash flow requirements.

The Nature and Context of Project Management

The project manager may well be asked to run 'what if' scenarios to test the impact of removing certain aspects of the deliverables or to determine the costs involved in terminating the project at this stage. This is much easier if computer software is being used. Assuming the project is to continue any changes must be dealt with and any corrective actions taken.

Corrective and Preventive Action

The project manager must co-ordinate the reports from task managers and analyse the information. The most effective approach to dealing with variances will depend on the situation, but it is usually best to pause and consider all the issues rather than leaping to an instant remedy. Review the project and try to understand why there is a variance and what options there are available. Evaluate the options, select the most appropriate and then get support from all stakeholders. Once an agreed form of response has been reached then take the action. Repeated changes and indecision at this point will cause confusion. The project schedule will need to be updated and any corrective and preventive action taken. Task owners must be kept up to date with any changes, particularly to the critical path and any changes in deliverables.

The project manager may identify possible problems ahead and must ensure that the task owner has appropriate recovery plans in place. He will continuously be reviewing the risk of success or failure of the project by analysing the cost and time estimates and the task network. A project simulation program may be used to try out different options. It can also produce a list of all the project tasks with their risk of being on the critical path, so a task with a 90% risk can be given more attention that one with a 10% risk. The manager can than take preventive actions to avoid or reduce the risks.

Project Final Report

The final review is often the project final report. It usually occurs at the end of a project when the goals have been achieved and the project is handed over to the operational side of the business (internal) or to the customer (external). However, it may also happen at an earlier stage when the project is prematurely terminated; for example when a project fails to reach a milestone or the money is withdrawn.

The Nature and Context of Project Management

For a small project the final report may be a short memo, but for a longer project the main items that should be included in a final report are:

- Overview of the project (including any changes to the original plan)
- Major goals achieved (compared with the goals identified at the start)
- Final accounts and analysis of variances to budget
- Performance evaluation of the system, team, contractors etc. This is very useful to future project managers selecting their team members
- Areas for improvement in the future
- Recommendations for approaches that worked
- Results of each phase (goals, budget, schedule etc)
- Executive summary.

Parts of the report may be confidential e.g. the accounts and the personnel performances. In some cases there may be a separate 'lessons learnt' report. This will help make future projects better, and is part of continuous improvement processes.

As well as writing the final report there are other activities that are carried out at the end of a project. These include:

- Disposal of any equipment or left over materials
- Re-assignment of personnel
- Transfer of responsibilities
- Finalisation of all accounts and contract details
- Customer satisfaction. Communication with the customer will have been maintained throughout the project to ensure that they are happy with the progress of the project and to check that they have not changed their minds. However, at the end of the project it is very instructive to ask the customer if they are satisfied and if they felt that any areas of the service could be improved. This can be done using a formal questionnaire, a phone call with a set of questions or other methods as might suit the industry. The customer's viewpoint is different from that of the team and may give useful feedback on how things can be improved in the future.

Finally, it is often the custom to celebrate the end of a project. The style will depend on the size of the project and the industry. This occasion plays a useful role in building up morale within the organisation.

The Nature and Context of Project Management

Project Audits

A Project Audit is a particular type of Project Review. The main purpose of an audit is to provide information on actual performance against pre-determined plans and standards. As part of the audit, a review can be undertaken which builds on the information and seeks to suggest ways that poor performance can be addressed to ensure success on the next project. Further, it ensures that the systems and procedures that were put in place for the execution of the project are being correctly followed, and also allows for corrective action to be taken if necessary. The emphasis should focus on improving the output from the project rather than simply increasing the rigour of the procedures.

The Audit Cycle

Define – What is the purpose of the audit?
Collect – Information
Assess – Compare what is actually happening against the plan. Are there discrepancies?
Identify Change – What improvements could be made? Maybe not on this project but in the future.

The most formal type of project audit is requested by the client. It is often used when the project is off-track and there is a need to get to the bottom of the problem. It is also common on government projects. The aim of this type of audit is to get an accurate picture of the quality of work, expenditure, and schedule. It is like a formal status report, but objective outsiders are usually the auditors.

The Nature and Context of Project Management

Section 4

Project Planning

Project Planning

Project Planning

Planning Concepts

Why bother with project planning?

"Projects need planning" Most people agree with this, but why is it that sometimes it does not get done? The normal excuses given for not planning include 'lack of time', 'no need for it', and 'it is too much effort'. However, it is definitely worth it and any time taken to plan will be more than made up for in the time saved during the project by getting things right first time.

Unplanned projects have some typical problems:

- Deadlines that cannot be met
- Unclear scope or objectives
- Unsatisfactory quality that added to cost
- No strategy/reason for doing the work
- Unclear roles and responsibilities
- Poor cost control

Whereas, there are some very clear benefits of planning:

- The process of planning the project can identify possible problems. Some problems might be so considerable that they would cause the project to fail and so raise the question as to whether the project should take place at all.
- It allows estimates of time and budget to be determined – again if these are unacceptable, the scope of the project can be reviewed to see if an alternate version of the project is more acceptable.
- After the planning process the resulting project has a much greater likelihood of success.
- The planning process helps align the resource requirements with the demands of the rest of the organisation. If team members are to be seconded to the project team it provides functional managers with an idea of when they will have to supply staff. If specialist plant or machinery is required then again it allows the functional manager in charge of the equipment to plan this requirement into his departmental schedule.
- The project plan provides an excellent communication device, allowing all the stakeholders to see what is needed and where they fit in.

Project Planning

- A project plan can be used to demonstrate commitment by asking all stakeholders to sign it. This can be a useful proof of commitment if dissent is expected later on during the project. For instance, if the plant manager refuses to given up time on the plant, then he can be reminded that he was aware of the need and agreed to it.
- The project plan can help clarify the objectives of the project. Does everyone agree with the objectives? This helps ensure that the result is actually what everybody expected.
- However, above all a plan puts a line in the sand and is the basis of the control of the project. It allows comparison of the current state with the expected state and so deviations can be seen and corrective actions taken.

Often the original plan is high-level and will be developed in greater detail as the project progresses and unknowns are clarified. Plans should look forward and be focused on things the project team have control of and responsibility for. The key elements of a plan will be time, costs, deliverables, quality, people and risk.

What should be included in the Project Plan? This will depend on the size of the project and for a small project this may only be a couple of pages. For a larger project the contents could be:

Introduction and Summary
- Name, issue number, date of issue, reference number
- List of contents
- Sponsor name (the project supporter – usually the financial supporter or customer)
- Project objectives and a brief overview of how they will be achieved by the project
- Overview of the completion criteria and acceptance measures – including key milestones and approval points
- List of amendments to the plan with a Work Breakdown Structure (WBS) reference including a brief description of the reasons for the amendments and date
- List of any policies, standards, and specifications covering the project e.g. Health and Safety, licences, permits etc
- Organisational diagram and methods of operation for financial management, change management, purchasing strategy, reporting structure etc.
- Circulation list and project directory

Project Planning

- Reference to the original authorisation of the project
- Assumptions made during the planning process
- Risk analysis results and insurance policy details

Commitment Acceptance
This lists the task owners' commitments and the Project Manager's acceptance of them. This may be a list of WBSs that have been signed off by the task owners. This section would also contain control documents such as budget releases, budget status and the change management documentation.

Project Work Breakdown Structure
This is the description of tasks in the project plan. A project WBS dictionary, with a short summary description of each task listed with its WBS reference.

Schedule of Work
This could be displayed as a GANTT chart and a network. It is useful to list all the deliverables by time and by task owner.

Statement of Work
The statement of work should include the specifications together with references to technical documents, etc. that may be needed.

Project Quality Plan
This will describe how the quality criteria included in the project objectives will be achieved. If the organisation is accredited to ISO9001 the quality manual will assist the project team in developing this plan.

Resource details
Resource details include manpower and skill requirements and equipment needs as well as all the materials and supplies for the project.

The Budget
The cost breakdown for the project, including key milestones for the release of tranches of funding and often the expected cash flow for the project.

Project Planning

Managing the planning process

The Planning process is shown in the Figure 4.1.

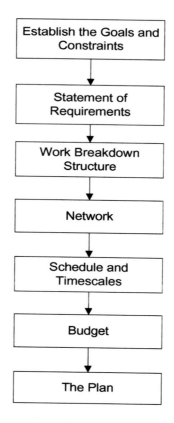

Figure 4.1 Flow diagram of a typical planning process

Each element in the planning process will now be considered in turn.

Goals, Constraints and Requirements

Goals or Objectives are important to project success. Unclear goals or objectives will lead to an unsatisfactory project that is likely to fail. In simple terms the goals are the specification of what must be achieved by the end of the project. All stakeholders should agree project goals; otherwise somebody is bound to be dissatisfied at the end of the project. The project goals should provide the criteria that are needed to measure success in

Project Planning

completing a project. The goals need to be reviewed regularly and consensus reached before moving onto the next phase of the project. Project scope is not the same as the project goal; it is the size of the project. It is the scope that defines the assumptions for making all the schedule and resource projections in the project planning. It puts boundaries on the planning process and the deliverables. The deliverables of the project must be identified. If work is added 'little by little' to the project this is known as scope 'creep'.

Risk Assessment

Even with clear goals established you should carry out a risk and constraint analysis that will help you establish whether the project goals that have been defined are feasible. Risk Assessment can also be used at other key stages in the project and can help greatly in bringing a project to successful conclusion. It ensures that the team is working to a common objective and that the constraints of the customer – cost, time, function, image etc and the prevailing physical and socio-political environment are acknowledged.

A structured risk management process can identify many of the risks and allow you to:

- Categorise the risk according to its type
- Assess the probability of a risk occurring and what impact it would have on the project
- Work out a suitable response to the risk and include some contingency planning
- Plan to share out the risks in the project, possibly to subcontractors or other stakeholders
- Take account of the risks now that they have been identified, and forewarned is forearmed

There are two types of risk, business risk and project risk.
Business Risk e.g. legislative changes, environmental issues, market changes. In the worst case the organisation might fail if any of these risks occur.
Project Risk e.g. failure of supplier, staff changes, technical problems. In the worst case the project would fail. This could also be enough to bring down the organisation if the project was significant enough.

Project Planning

Risk can also be classified depending on where the control is:

- Unpredictable and external e.g. acts of God, government actions, war
- Predictable, external and uncertain e.g. market prices for raw materials, weather
- Technical and internal e.g. design issues
- Non-technical and internal e.g. staff issues

In identifying risks, brainstorming sessions with the project team can be very useful. Past experience on similar projects can show what can go wrong and in large projects computer modelling allows several "what if" situations to be evaluated. Once all the possible risks have been identified then each should be assessed. Estimate its effect on the project – say on a scale of 1 – 10 with 10 being the highest impact. Estimate how likely it is to happen – again on a scale of 1 – 10 with 10 being the highest probability. Multiplying the two factors together gives a quantified risk. Once identified the results should be reviewed with all stakeholders. There are four basic options for dealing with risk:

- Do nothing special – deal with it if it happens. This is an appropriate strategy if the cost of trying to eliminate the risk is higher than the cost of dealing with it when it arrives.
- Avoid it – change the project to delete that part of it that contained the risk. Make sure though, that without this section the project still makes sense.
- Monitor it – and develop a contingency plan. It is better to proactively manage risk as soon as the problem starts than not see it until it is too late to do anything.
- Transfer the risk – insurance or subcontracting e.g. a fixed price contract with a supplier transfers the risk of cost increases to the supplier.

In some cases the risks may be so high that the project is not allowed to proceed. In other cases the deliverables are changed to allow less risk to be inherent (e.g. using a more standard technology). Assuming the project is given the go ahead, it is the project manager's job to offset or manage the risk. The entire risk management analysis and risk management plan should be documented and form part of the project plan. This plan should not only include measures for dealing with problems that might occur, but also who is responsible for doing it. Risk management is not solely concerned with avoiding risk but of assessing and managing the uncertainties that exist.

Project Planning

As well as looking at the risk of the whole project, there are risk analysis techniques that are useful at different stages of the project. In particular, during the design phase of the project, Failure Mode and Effects Analysis can play a key role. It can identify risks in the final deliverables at a stage in the project where corrections can be done.

Project Constraints

The constraints on a project, unlike the risks are known in advance and projects are typically constrained by:

- Money – how much do you have for the project?
- Schedule – what is the delivery date you must meet, are you waiting for another project to finish?
- People – do you have the right skills in your team?
- Facilities and Equipment – are they available at the right time?

The constraints should be well documented in the project statement of work; they can limit what can be achieved on the project.

Work Breakdown Structure and Networking

Work Breakdown Structure has been described in Section 3. The theory and practice of Networking is covered later on in this Section.

Scheduling and Timescales

Scheduling and Timescales are covered under the PERT and Critical Path Analysis heading later on in this Section.

Budget

A budget is a list of estimated or expected expenditures for the project along with how they are to be financed. Budgets give the management a plan for expenditure of the organisation's resources e.g. money and time, during the course of the project.

$$\text{RESOURCES (including PEOPLE)} + \text{TIME} = \text{BUDGET}$$

Project Planning

There are six basic resources required to carry out most projects.

- People – availability, skill, rate of pay, quality
- Equipment – availability, cost etc.
- Facilities – factory availability etc
- Money – how much is there for the project? Are the sponsors trying to build a luxury car for the cost of a small car?
- Materials and supplies – estimates must be gathered from suppliers. Renting might be considered rather than buying if the items are only needed for a short time. If possible three bids should be received and negotiation may reduce the price. The suppliers' quality must be assessed – do they have ISO9001 accreditation?
- Technology – is the latest technology to be used? Is it robust?

Resource choices will affect the quality, budget and schedule for the project. If the resources needed are only available at a certain date, then the programme will need to be adapted to account for this. The availability of as many as possible of the required resources should be checked before the project is approved.

People

The most important resource for the project is arguably the project team. Once the tasks have been reviewed and the people resource identified, then the people profiles can be built up. What skills and experiences are needed for each task? The plan should take advantage of each team member's skills and accommodate their weaknesses. The questions that need answering include:

- What skills are required?
- Where will the people come from (seconded, recruited etc.)?
- How should they be organised (functional, project or matrix structure)?

The human resource department may be able to help in identifying the people with the skills and experience needed. This will certainly be the case if they follow the requirements of Investors in People or ISO9001: 2000. These standards require training evaluations to be carried out and training records maintained. Of course there may not be a choice of people, in this case additional training will be required and 'outside' contractors can be used to fill–in the missing skills and experience. Contractors can also be used to 'speed' up projects, but at the expense of increasing the budget.

Project Planning

Other balancing could include swapping an inexperienced person (cheap but slower) with an experienced person (more expensive, but could get the job done more quickly).

Whether work is assigned to people or people assigned to work will probably depend on the policy of the organisation. If work is assigned to people, then the project team is formed first and work assigned to people in the team. In this case there is a risk that the skills of the team may not be appropriate to the work. Alternatively, the scope of work can be defined first and then a project team is formed with the appropriate skills to deliver the project.

Costs

The processes required to ensure that the correct budget is assigned to the project are:
- Cost estimating – the cost of the resources needed to complete the project activities (some of which will have been identified at the resource identification stage).
- Cost budgeting – allocating the overall cost estimate to individual work packages.

Cost estimates are usually expressed in currencies, but other units such as staff hours, or days may be used and then translated into currencies later. There are several established methods for budgeting: top down, bottom up and parametric modelling.

Bottom up

The cost of each individual work package is estimated and then they are all added together to get the total budget.

Project Planning

Top down

This approach uses the actual cost of a previous similar project, or senior management experience as to what the project is likely to cost and this is divided down among the tasks. It is more difficult to achieve an accurate budget using this approach, but it is much quicker than the bottom up approach and so is usually used in the early phases of a project. In both methods information on costs can be obtained from a variety of places e.g. previous project files, commercial cost estimating databases, previous project team knowledge etc.

Parametric Modeling

Parametric modelling can also be useful – this is a mathematical model that uses project characteristics to compute total project costs e.g. if office blocks cost £2000/m^2 floor area and the planned office block has a 10,000m^2 floor area, then the budget will be £20 million.

These type of models can be accurate if:
- The projects are similar
- The historical data used to build the model was accurate
- The model is scalable. It assumes that all costs are proportional to core costs.

The costs within the model are based on an average of estimates of core costs, vendor quotes and the prices of placed orders gathered from projects over a period of time.

There is often a reluctance to use figures from a database, as the assumptions behind them may not be understood and there can be a preference to use figures that have been personally sourced or used before.

Project Planning

Types of Estimate

There are various types of estimate with varying accuracy and their appropriateness depends on the project stage.

Type of Estimate	Typical Range of Accuracy	Purpose
Order of magnitude – "rough cut"	-25% to +75%	Initial evaluation of project
Budget	-10% to +25%	Establish funds required and apply for project approval
Definitive	-5% to 10%	Bid proposals, contracts, baseline for budget control of the project

Table 4.1 Types of Estimate

The cost budgeting stage then allocates the cost estimates to the individual work packages and establishes a cost baseline for measuring performance. The budget should help the project manager control the projects – not the other way around.

When preparing an estimate of the costs for a budget, everything needed for the successful completion of the project must be included. Anything required, but not included in the budget, will cause an overspend. Items to include in the budget are:

- Labour – the main project team and also people who will not be part of the project team, but may still be doing work for the project. This is often initially included as man-hours and translated by the finance department using their standard 'person' cost. Whether this includes an overhead loading (i.e. a share of non-productive labour employed by the organisation) depends on the norms of the organisation – but it is an assumption that should be included in the attachment to the budget.
- Travel and expenses – the project team may need to visit suppliers, project sites etc.
- Training – for the team and for the end users.

Project Planning

- Material – this is not just the parts required for manufacture but also any parts required for the prototype, consumables used in the project including stationery etc.
- Plant and Equipment – purchase of specialist plant or hiring of standard plant from another division etc.
- Consultants and Subcontractors – the cost of using specialist consultants or subcontract labour.
- Management – the cost of managing the project such as the cost of the project manager or team leaders. If a manager carries out the management as part of his ordinary duties, what % of time will he be booking to the project?
- Overheads – the costs of these will depend on how the organisation deals with overheads. Are they spread into the labour rate of productive staff or must they be included as a separate item?
- Inflation – particularly if the project will take several years.
- Contingencies – this may be added as a standard percentage. This would include exchange rate risk if parts are being bought from overseas. The contingency factor will be higher if the risks are higher.
- Legal fees – if any legal support is needed e.g. contract documents.
- Marketing and advertising – for product announcements, literature etc.

The assembled budget must be tied to the project goals and these must be clearly understood. Designing a new car is obviously not a sufficient goal – what is needed are the specifications it must meet, the final target selling price, maintenance costs etc. These will all impact the cost of the project – as will the amount of risk the management are willing to take. A high-risk project using new technology is much more likely to overspend than one using tried and tested technology. Costs are also tied to time frames, making a project deliver more quickly can increase costs because 'rush' charges and overtime may need paying.

Project Planning

The Final Plan

All these elements are put together to form the project plan. After the planning, the project has to be carried out. In most projects there is a kick-off meeting with the project team. Getting the project started right means COMMUNICATING. The kick-off meeting maybe the first opportunity for the project team to meet each other and to see the final complete plan. The idea of this meeting is to motivate the team, make sure that everybody knows what has to be done and when it has to be done by.

The kick–off meeting should:

- Explain the project goals to all team members and make sure they all know their own objectives and responsibilities for the project
- Generate enthusiasm and commitment for the project
- Identify critical deadlines and phases of the project
- Explain the reporting structure and who is in charge
- Review the schedule and work plan (the budget may be confidential)
- Explain the operating procedure e.g. reports required, the meeting schedule and the communication routes
- Issue a project directory
- Start the project

Planning does not finish as soon as the project starts, it is on-going as the situation changes. (See Project Control and Review).

Networking

Network diagram: a logical representation of tasks that defines the sequence of work in a project. It shows the workflow and not just the work. Networks are usually drawn from left to right or top to bottom with lines drawn between tasks to show precedence i.e. the order that tasks have to be done. They are not as good as WBSs at showing hierarchical relationships, but are very useful for scheduling tasks. In most large project both WBS and networking will be used for managing the project.

Project Planning

The following definitions are used in sorting out precedence in the network.

- Mandatory dependencies – those that are inherent in the nature of the work being done e.g. in construction you have to lay the foundations before building the walls. These dependencies are often called 'Hard Logic'.
- Discretionary dependencies – defined by the project team e.g. activities are sequenced to meet "best practice" requirements, where it is best to do things in a certain order. These are often called 'Soft Logic'. Activities constrained by availability of a unique resource are called 'preferential logic.
- External dependencies – interfaces to other projects or events e.g. a prototype must be available for a trade show.
- Leads and Lags. A lag is the amount of time after one task is started or finished before the next task can be started or finished. Lead is the amount of time that precedes the start of work on another task.
- Precedence – defines the task sequencing order and how tasks are related in the plan e.g. if a task has to be completed before the next task can start, the first task takes precedence over the second. Network diagrams are sometimes called precedence diagrams.
- Simultaneous activities – some tasks can happen at the same time, as long as there is the resource available.

To create a Network diagram:

- The task list or WBS is used to identify all the tasks – each task is given a number or code to identify it uniquely.
- Identify the relationship between tasks. To assist in this the following questions can be asked:
    What task must precede this task?
    What tasks follow this task?
    What tasks can be worked on together?
  A simple list can be used to note the precedence and dependencies.
- Any milestones required are identified. Milestones are not tasks; they can be used for summarising work that has been completed. Milestones for the project could be the top levels in the WBS.
- The tasks and milestones are laid out as a network. There are computer programmes for doing this, but smaller projects can be done by hand, for example by using a white board and sticky notes.

Project Planning

- The network logic is reviewed.
    Check that all tasks are present and properly sequenced
    Is all the precedence and dependencies correct?
    Are all the simultaneous tasks correct, are there others that have been missed?
    Will the completion of the tasks in the network deliver the project?

Changing the precedence or the parallel activities alters the resources and the time needed to do the project. The goal in developing the network diagram is to identify activities that can occur simultaneously and specify the precedence among all the activities. This should lead to the development of an optimum sequence of tasks and show the Critical Path (the shortest path) through the project.

Activity on Node (AoN)

This is a method of constructing a network diagram using nodes to represent the activities that are connected with arrows to show dependencies. It is the method used by most software packages for project management. It is based on four precedence relationships:

- Start to start: the "from" activity must start before the "to" activity can start.
- Finish to finish: the "from" activity must be finished before the "to" activity can finish.
- Finish to start: the "from" activity must be finished before the "to" activity can start.
- Start to finish: the "from" activity must start before the "to" activity can finish.

Finish-to-start dependency is the most common. Start-to-start and finish-to-finish are also found and allow overlap of succeeding activities in time. This allows fast-tracking of projects. Start-to-finish is rarely used.

Project Planning

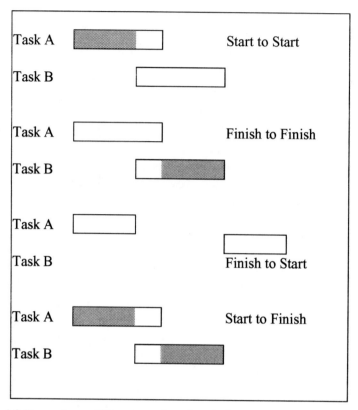

Figure 4.2 Precedence Diagramming for AoN Networks

AoN networks are becoming more widely used than the alternative Activity on Arrow networks because:
- It is easy to associate work with a box
- It is easier to draw the network. Each activity has a box and the logic dependencies can be inserted later
- It is easier to write the software
- You don't have to use dummy activities.

Project Planning

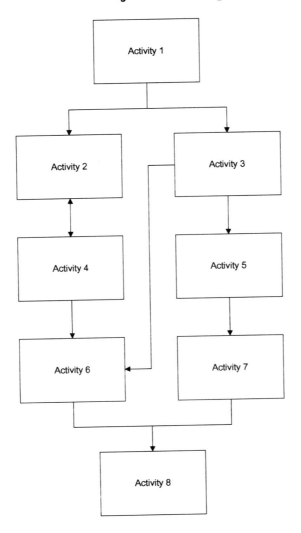

Example AON Network
The Nodes are the activities and the arrows show the precedence relationship

Figure 4.3 An Example AoN Network

Project Planning

Activity on Arrow (AoA)

In this method of diagramming, arrows are used to represent activities and they are connected at nodes to show dependencies. This method only uses 'finish – to – start' dependencies and may need the use of dummy activities to define all logical relationships correctly. An arrow goes from one event to another only if the first event is the immediate predecessor of the second. If an event has to wait for another event, but there is no activity between the two events then the two events are joined with a dotted arrow to show a dummy activity.

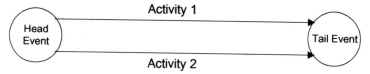

Incorrect - Violates Rule

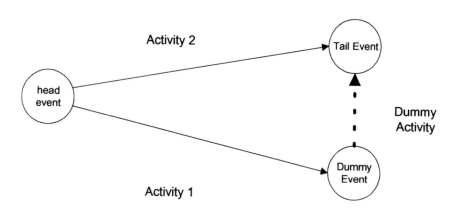

Add Dummy Event and Activity

Figure 4.5 Adding a dummy event to an AoA Network

Project Planning

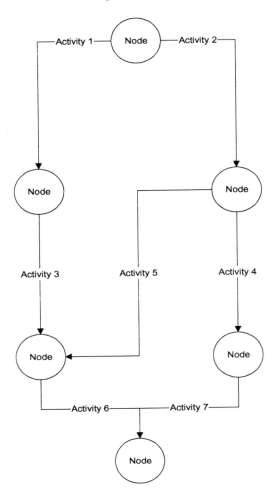

Figure 4.6 Example AoA Network. The arrows are the activities and the nodes are events.

Conditional diagramming methods e.g. GERT (Graphical Evaluation and Review Technique) allow for loops and conditional branches that are not allowed in AoN or AoA.

Project Planning

PERT and Critical Path Analysis

A **PERT chart** is an event orientated project network diagram. PERT and CPA are often used interchangeably, but the former should only really apply when the network is used to track process.

Critical Path Analysis is a technique for establishing the time needed for a project and what the critical activities are. CPA gives an early and late start and finish date for each activity on the network. As its name suggests, it calculates the float and determines those activities that have the least flexibility, giving the critical path for the project. It concentrates on the single objective, that of managing time using the critical path.

The difference between PERT and CPA is in the way information is displayed and how scheduling uncertainties are dealt with. In CPA, one time estimate is used for creating the schedule, PERT uses a more complex system based on three time estimates that are used to find the most probable completion time. AOA or AON can be used to represent activities and events in the PERT/CPA networks. Essentially, the PERT/CPA techniques allow the networking and precedence technique to be added to the scheduling methods, such that completion times can be found.

Notation

In AoN networks, each work element is depicted using a box like the one shown below. This notation is sometimes called PERT notation.

early start	duration	early finish
Description/Activity No.		
late start	float	late finish

The earliest date that the activity can start is known as the early start date. The early start date plus the duration is the early finish date. There is also a date by which it could finish and not delay the project – this is known as the late finish date. The late finish date less the duration is known as the late start date. The available float is the late start date less the early start date. If the float is zero then this is a critical task. Tasks with very small floats are called near critical activities.

Project Planning

As an example let us look at four activities

Activity	Duration
Activity 1	2 days
Activity 2	7 days
Activity 3	19 days
Activity 4	5 days

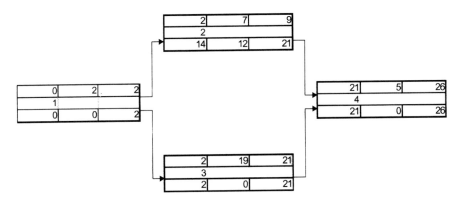

Figure 4.4 Example network using PERT notation

Calculate the early start and finish dates by doing a 'forward pass' through the network. Calculate the late start and finish dates by doing a 'back pass' through the network. The critical path in this simple example is 1,3,4 as there is no float.

Time Schedule

Time tends to be seen as the most important element in managing the project, but although being late reduces the benefits, it does not usually cause a project to fail completely.

There are 3 main types of constraint that will influence the development of the time schedule.

- Imposed dates e.g. market launch linked to a major trade show
- Major milestones. For example, deliverables required by the project e.g. opening a re-furbished department within a store in time for Christmas
- Assumptions, if they do not come true then there will be problems to iron out.

Project Planning

The first stage in developing the time schedule is to use the WBS to identify the tasks. Then a network diagram is used to give the logical sequence, and the addition of time-scales to a plan turns it into a schedule and CPA can be used to identify the critical path.

In it's most basic form a time schedule just contains the planned start and finish dates and duration of each activity. It may also indicate if there is any flexibility in the start date. As the project progresses the planned start and finish dates are updated with actual dates and the resultant impact on the overall schedule can be seen. As seen earlier, an activity that has no flexibility or float is a critical element and the route through the project encompassing the critical items is the critical path. As a project progresses the critical path can change and different activities may become critical.

Applying timescales to each WBS means estimating how long the task will take. The time taken to complete an activity is not necessarily the effort required to complete the work. Time is usually used to denote the duration of the activity from start to finish. Effort is the number of man hours needed. For example, acquiring a piece of equipment may take 4 hours of effort in locating and ordering it, but the duration may be 10 days, because it takes 10 days to be delivered. Duration can also be less than the man-hours required if several people are working on the project.

$$\text{Duration} = \frac{\text{Work content (man days)}}{\text{No. of people available}}$$

But how do you estimate the amount of time and effort needed for an activity? Typically the project manager makes an estimate – which is often only a stab in the dark and project schedules based entirely on this approach will usually lead to significant problems in controlling the project. The accuracy of the estimate is dependent on the level of experience of the person making the 'guess', the familiarity of the type of activity and the amount of knowledge about the factors that will influence the time taken. The more knowledge available then the more accurate the estimate is likely to be. Thus, if the scope of the project is not clearly defined, then the estimates are likely to be less accurate – if you don't know what you have to achieve, how can you tell how long it will take?

Project Planning

There are some approaches that can help with estimating time.

- Expert Judgement – people who are experienced in the area pool their knowledge and arrive at an agreed estimate. The estimate will still only be as good as the experts chosen and everyone must be allowed to have their say. (A strong character can exert peer pressure that distorts the estimates of others, since they do not wish to disagree with him.) This technique is also called the Delphi technique – after the oracle at Delphi.
- Previous Experience – past data on similar projects is very valuable for estimating future costs and timescales. Some organisations, whose business is project management for clients, have departments who take the results from past projects and enter them into a database and this is used when estimating future projects.
- Top down estimates - take the whole project and then break it down into stages based upon delivery and major decision points. The time for each of these major stages is estimated and then they are all summed to get an overall estimate. This is often done at the feasibility stage, and then at each stage within the project where the estimates can be refined and should become more accurate.
- Bottom up estimates - this is the opposite of top-down. Each activity of the project is identified and a time estimate given to it. This should be easier to carry out since the activities will be small and may well have been carried out on another project. However, there is a danger of over-estimating. If every activity has had a contingency built in, by the time all of them have been added together you may have an unneeded amount of contingency. This technique is usually used at the detailed planning stage of the project.
- Standard Product Method - this method is most commonly used on products that are regularly produced. A matrix is developed of standard types of product against time based on historical information, the more information the greater the degree of accuracy. When a new product is planned the matrix is used to estimate the time required by identifying the most appropriate intersection on the matrix,

Whatever method is used, an estimate is just an estimate and the project manager should not rely on finishing exactly on time. The planned date is the date the activity is planned to start – set sometime between the early start date and the late start date and dependent on factors such as the availability of resource. The baseline date is the planned date at the start of the project, whilst the scheduled date is the planned date on the current schedule. The

Project Planning

estimates should be updated as the project progresses and the information available increases.

In estimating an activity's duration you must also take into account that people will not be working full time on that activity. If an activity is to take 10 man-days, it doesn't mean that Mr Smith will finish it in two weeks. The hours spent by Mr Smith on this project will unlikely to be 100% of his time. A schedule that assumes that everybody spends 100% of their time on the project is unrealistic and will lead to problems. Reasons for not spending 100% on the project include: attendance at team meetings, communicating with colleagues and unscheduled interruptions e.g. a panic call from a client requiring immediate attention. To allow for these reductions in working time available to the project, the project manager may need to adjust the timing by factoring in a loss factor. Taking into account holidays, sickness, training, group meeting etc it has been estimated that a person assigned 100% to a project actually only spends 70% of his time on the project, thus you need to adjust the durations to account for this. There is also another side to this – if the project staff are constantly working 'overtime' but this is not included in the costing, then the reporting is falsely recording the actual time for the job. This could mean that future projects are under resourced because a false level of resource has been recorded in an earlier project. Further, inexperienced staff may take longer than experienced staff, and so although a 'Standard Person' may be used, the time will have to be adjusted if a more experienced or less experienced person carries out the activity.

Another factor to be aware of is padding. As seen earlier it is preferable not to add padding for contingencies to each task; this can build up to total an unnecessarily large element. Instead a general contingency, often between 2-7% of the project time can be added at the end.

Gantt Charts

There are two typical ways of communicating a project's time schedule.

- Activity listings
- Gantt charts

Activity Listings can include an immense amount of detail and although this is useful at the detailed planning stages, it is easier to get an overall picture of the project using graphical representations.

Project Planning

A **Gantt chart** is the most common form of graphical representation. The activities are listed down the left hand side and their timing and duration march across the page. A line on the Gantt chart shows the date each task begins and ends based on its precedence and duration.

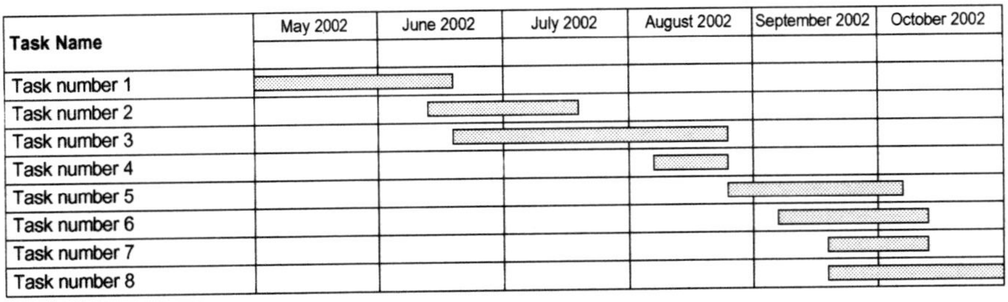

Task Name	May 2002	June 2002	July 2002	August 2002	September 2002	October 2002
Task number 1	▭▭▭▭					
Task number 2		▭▭▭				
Task number 3			▭▭▭▭			
Task number 4				▭▭		
Task number 5					▭▭▭▭	
Task number 6					▭▭▭▭	
Task number 7						▭▭▭
Task number 8						▭▭▭

Figure 4.7 A Simple GANTT Chart

Note that GANTT charts do not generally show interrelationships between tasks, the network diagram is needed for this; although the critical path can be indicated and dependency links added.

Milestone charts. GANTT charts are often modified to give additional information. For instance, milestones are added. The milestone symbol shows an event rather than an activity – it does not use any time or resources. GANTT charts changed in this way are often called "milestones charts".

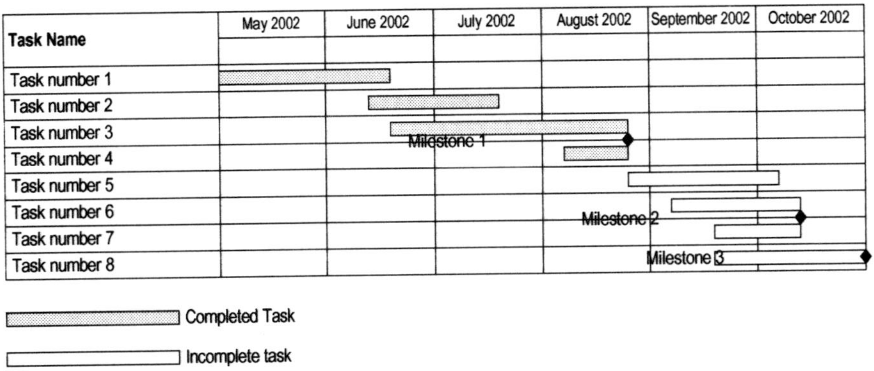

Task Name	May 2002	June 2002	July 2002	August 2002	September 2002	October 2002
Task number 1	▭▭▭▭					
Task number 2		▭▭▭				
Task number 3			Milestone 1 ◆			
Task number 4				▭▭		
Task number 5					▭▭▭▭	
Task number 6				Milestone 2 ◆		
Task number 7					▭▭▭	
Task number 8					Milestone 3 ◆	

▭▭▭ Completed Task
▭▭▭ Incomplete task

Figure 4.8 A Simple Milestone chart

Project Planning

Gantt Charts and milestone charts can be changed to include other information, such as task responsibility, reasons for delay and planned action.

PERT / CPA Scheduling

GANTT charts have limited schedule analysis capabilities and any large-scale projects will need greater planning and coordinating of the numerous activities and this is where PERT and CPA are used. As mentioned earlier, although they were originally different because of their approach to time estimating, today they really comprise one technique.

Project scheduling using PERT_CPA has four basic phases:

- Planning
- Scheduling
- Improvement
- Controlling

As before, the project is broken down into activities (WBS), each activity has a time estimate given to it and then a network diagram is used to determine the order of tasks, before entering the information into the programme. This type of software programme is used not only to plan but also to control the project.

As we have seen, the critical path is a sequence of tasks that form the shortest duration for the project. If a task is delayed on the critical path, then the whole project will be delayed. Tasks not lying on the critical path will have more flexibility and once the schedule has been developed, then it can be improved, e.g. bottlenecks identified and managed. The tasks to concentrate on improving are those in the critical path, since any improvement in them will reduce the overall time for the project. The project can be controlled via the programme as each task status can be updated and the overall effect on the project seen. The project manager can also use the programme to try out different scenarios before deciding on the best action to bring the project back into line. It can be used to evaluate the effects of changes in requirements, schedule, resources etc. The network should be seen as a 'moving' schedule that needs to be revised as conditions change. The common causes of slippage are poor planning and poor management of the project. Reviews should be held at intervals frequent enough to assure that any problems are seen before schedule slippage becomes a real concern.

Project Planning

It is usually possible to compress project schedules if you are willing to pay the additional costs. If we assume that there is a straight line relationship between the cost of performing an activity on a normal schedule and the cost of performing the activity on a 'crash' schedule, there is a point beyond which no further time can be saved, then for a given activity the cost per unit of time saved is:

$$\frac{\text{Crash cost} - \text{Normal cost}}{\text{Normal time} - \text{Crash time}}$$

To decide which of the activities on the critical path should be 'crashed', take a look at this calculation. Once the activity has been 'crashed', the programme must be re-run to find out what the new critical path is. One should not assume speeding up a project would just add costs. Although the direct costs will increase, the indirect costs (overheads etc) will go down if the total time for the project is reduced. There is actually a breakeven point when the indirect costs (which go down as the project time decreases) are added to the direct costs (which increase as the project is crashed). This is shown in Figure 4.9.

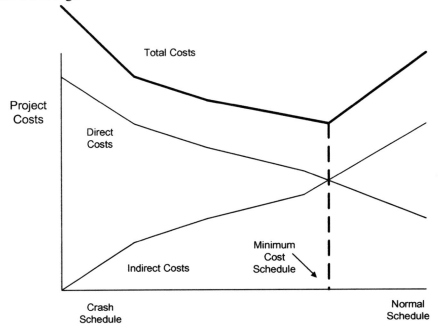

Figure 4.9 Total costs vs Project Duration

Project Planning

The project schedule developed will probably require many revisions, both during the planning stage and once the project is running. There must be a document control process in place so that all members of the team are working to the most recent version of the schedule. A document control register giving versions and issue status as used in a quality system can be a vital tool here.

Section 5

Quality in Project Management

Quality in Project Management

Quality in Project Management

Why have Quality Assurance in Projects?

As identified earlier there is a difference between Operational Management and Project Management in an organisation. In the case of operational management the same things happen over and over again and consequently it is possible to learn to get it right, after enough mistakes! However, with Project Management – where new things happen - is there the same opportunity to improve over time and learn from our mistakes? Yes, the project process is the same even if the application is very different.

A recent study of one of the country's leading project management organisations revealed:

- Poor understanding of customer requirements.
- Poor assessment and management of risk.
- Poor document control.

Another study of failing or failed projects revealed:

- Poor control of communication (interfaces) between client and contractors.
- Poor understanding of customer requirements.
- Poor project planning (in some cases amazingly - the promised delivery date was before the date the Contract Review Meeting (Order Acceptance) was carried out).
- Little or no risk analysis.

Thus, there is plenty of opportunity to improve project performance through quality assurance techniques.

In looking at 'quality' in project management we are not only concerned with the 'quality' of the final product, but also the 'quality' of the process of the project management. For example, the product quality may be excellent – delivering the product on time, on budget and with a satisfied customer, but if to achieve this, the project team had to work weekends and had many late evenings then this can lead to employee dissatisfaction. In this case the process was poor and needs to be identified as such so that it is not repeated in future projects. If it happens too often then the staff can become so dissatisfied they may leave! From the organisation's point of view this means that future projects may not be carried out as well, as experience from these staff has been lost.

Quality in Project Management

The project team should also remember that quality means meeting the requirements of the customer (internal or external), and high quality does not have to mean very expensive. Grade is used to define something that has extra facilities e.g. a Rolls Royce rather than a Ford – but both can be of high quality if they meet requirements. The team should understand and ensure that the project meets the requirements of both quality and grade.

Quality: The totality of features and characteristics of a product or service that bear on its ability to satisfy stated or implied needs - in simple terms this means Fitness for Purpose. Need covers more than mere function. Even if aesthetics is included in function there are many other factors to be considered. For example, the method of distribution, initial and running costs, user awareness or knowledge, other possible uses including reasonable misuse.

Grade: An indicator of category or rank related to features or characteristics that cover different sets of needs for products or services intended for the same functional use.

Grade	Quality	
	Good	Bad
High Grade	Gold pen that works perfectly	Gold pen that is unreliable
Low Grade	Ordinary plastic pen that writes smoothly	Ordinary plastic pen that doesn't write smoothly

Table 5.1 Quality vs. Grade

Quality vs. Grade: Table 5.1 above illustrates the difference between quality and grade. Both high grade (gold) and low grade (plastic) pens can be of high quality, if they meet the customer's expectations. Equally the pens can be low quality if they fail to meet the required customer standard. Another example of the misunderstanding of the difference between quality and grade is shown in the following quotation

Quality in Project Management

A carpenter once said, "This quality thing is all well and good when I perform work on Board Rooms finished with Oak panelling. But, I also fit out shops - down to a price - possibly using plastic fixtures and fittings. Now if quality means that the boardroom finish has to be put into shop fitting then that will put me out of business. No one will be able to afford my work".

Here the carpenter confused quality and grade, although the board room is a high grade job, both jobs need to achieve the correct quality, finished on time and to the agreed price.

Project Quality Management Processes

The main project quality management processes are:

- Quality Planning – which standards are relevant to the project and how will they be satisfied, e.g. if the organisation is accredited to ISO9001: 2000 then the project processes must satisfy this standard. The organisation's quality manual will contain requirements for meeting this standard together with any forms and record requirements the project will need to follow.
- Quality Control – looking at the results of the project processes, checking that they meet any relevant standards and seeing how to remove any causes of unsatisfactory performances.
- Quality Assurance – the project performance will be reviewed regularly to check that it will meet the relevant standards.

If the organisation has ISO9001 accreditation then Internal and External Auditors will undertake regular audits. They will audit the project and check that it is following the quality processes required.

The three processes outlined may not be as well defined as shown here, and may overlap and interact. However, each process will usually happen at least once in each phase of the project.

Quality in Project Management

Many of the project quality management activities are already included in general project management, e.g. reviews. This is how it should be, quality assurance should be embedded in the normal processes, it should not be seen as an 'extra'. However, as the project is usually of a temporary nature, any investments in improving the process may well have to be borne by the organisation and will be relevant for future projects since there is often not time for them to be implemented on the current project.

Quality Planning

Quality is planned in NOT inspected in. Thus right from the start of the project planning process, quality should be planned in. Usually, the project follows the quality policy of the organisation, but if several organisations are involved in the project, for instance in a joint venture, then a policy may need to be written for the project. At the end of the project planning phase the team will have a plan that should include requirements for quality management planning. The quality plan may be embedded within the overall project plan or may be a separately identified plan. The quality management plan must address quality control, quality assurance and quality improvement for the project.

Quality Plan

Every stage of a process or project is a possible source of poor quality; the objective of a Quality Plan is to anticipate possible sources of poor quality and to arrange the means of identifying such failures and preventing them from occurring.

A Quality Plan tends to be a project or product specific document that defines the Quality Assurance tasks to ensure that specific customer requirements and time scales are met. It allows anticipation of any project or product risk areas and gives the opportunity to take appropriate preventive/corrective action to eliminate or mitigate any such difficulties. This differs from a Quality Manual that is project or product independent and a Quality Programme that usually describes the implementation of the Quality Manual.

A Quality Plan identifies any existing and additional procedures or activities that may be necessary. For instance, on large capital cost projects such as construction projects or the launch of a new product or software development etc. - the main contractors can use it to control the activities of

Quality in Project Management

sub-contractors. It can be used as a model or a method of describing the Quality Assurance activities so that everyone can comment on, criticise and develop the plan ensuring their involvement in project achievement.

Normally the project manager or project controller is responsible for the generation of the Quality Plan; the plan would then require approval by the project team and possibly the customer.

Guidelines for Quality Planning

How to complete a Quality Control Plan:

The sequence to follow in the compilation of a Quality Control Plan for a project is given below.

- Identify the processes and ensure that there are adequate resources to complete the processes satisfactorily in terms of:
  Labour (quantity, skills, ability etc.)
  Facilities (equipment, assets, buildings etc.)
  Time
  Budget
  Materials
- Draw the project as a flow chart. Include all stages and activities.
- Transfer the flow chart onto the Quality Control Plan Form showing the following information:

1. Number and description of each stage.
2. The appropriate quality control activities associated with each stage; trials, design reviews, project reviews, tests etc. and when in the project sequence such quality control activities should take place.

Quality in Project Management

3. Source of Information: Description of the source of information for the person performing the task e.g. Quality Manual, Work Instruction Number 1234 etc. (The work instruction would need to include: the activity or task description, the sequence, the resources necessary to perform the task i.e. quantity of people, skills, materials, equipment (both process and measuring), the process standard and tolerance to be achieved.

   i. *Responsibility*: Who is responsible for performing the task?
   ii. *Record*: What records (if any) will be maintained showing successful completion of the task.
   iii. *Check by*: Who carries out (if anyone) the check on the task confirming successful completion and what inspection and records will be maintained of this check?
   iv. *Overseen by*: Who oversaw (or audited or reviewed) the check of the task confirming successful completion and what inspection and records were maintained of this check?)

- Re-assess the process or project commitments in the light of the information gained from the review of the necessary resource availability, the creation of the flow chart and the quality plan. Gain agreement and approval of the overall process or project quality plan from the project team members, key managers and customers.

Figure 5.1 is an example of a Quality Control Plan Flow Chart for a Software Process.

Quality in Project Management

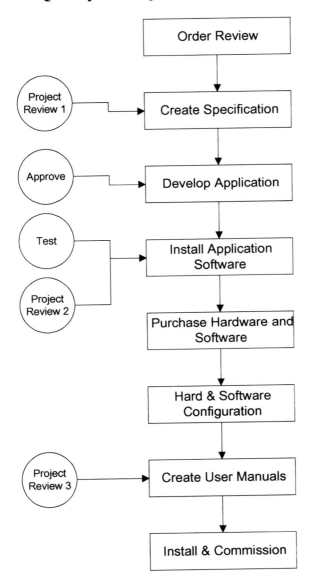

Figure 5.1 Flow Chart Software Project

The flowchart starts with a review of the order – this could be an internal order from the organisation or an external order from the client. Having accepted the order the specification is detailed and the project reviewed. The software application is then developed and approved. On completion of the software development the software is installed and tested. Following

Quality in Project Management

successful testing of the software the project is again reviewed. The proprietary hardware and software is purchased and the developed software integrated with it. The user and maintenance manuals are created and a final project review is conducted prior to final installation and commissioning on the customer's site.

With the completion of the flow chart the quality plan can be developed. Table 5.2 shows the development of the Flow Chart into a full Quality Plan. The plan includes:

- A detailed description of the various stages.
- Quality criteria and reference documents that contain the procedures to be observed.
- The responsibilities for observing the procedures and the records to be maintained.
- Identification of the responsibilities for approvals.

Quality Plan							
Client Name:		Plan Description:			Prepared by:	
Client Order Number:					Approved by:	
Client Address:		Plan Number:			Date of Issue:	
Client Telephone/Fax Number:						
#	Stage Description	Quality Criteria	Reference Documents	Responsibility	Record	Approvals	
							Org	Customer
I.	Order Acceptance	Contract Review	Order review procedure	Project Manager	Order File	DR100%	
Project Mobilisation							
II.	Create Contract Specific Project & Quality Plan	Design/ Project Input	Standard Project Plan Format	Project Manager	Project Plan	DR100%	
III.	Project Review 1	Design/ Project Verification	Project Review Minutes Check List	Project Manager	Project Review Minutes		

Quality in Project Management

			Develop Application Software				
IV.	Develop Prototype Application Specification	Design/ Project Input	Standard Application Specification Format	Project Manager	Application Specification	DR100%	
V.	Create Acceptance Specification	Design/ Project Input	Standard Acceptance Specification Format	Project Manager	Acceptance Specification	DR100%	
VI.	Develop Application Software	Design/ Project Process	Codes of Practice Application Development	Programmers	Code	DR10 (sample)	
VII.	Install Application Software in house. Records of acceptance will be shown on the Acceptance Specification document, copy retained of acceptance in project file	Design/ Project Process	Codes of Practice for Installation	Programmer	Acceptance Specification	DR100%	
VIII.	Acceptance of Application Software. Records of acceptance will be shown on the Acceptance Specification	Design/ Project Verification		Programmer	Acceptance Specification	DA (ind)	
IX.	Project Review 2	Design/ Project Verification	Project Review Minutes Check List	Project Manager	Project Review Minutes		

Quality in Project Management

			Hardware & Software Procurement				
X.	Purchase Proprietary Hardware & Software	Purchasing Control	Hardware & Software Schedules Approved Supplier List	Purchasing	Purchase Order	DA	
XI.	Hardware & Software delivered	Verification	Quality Manual	Goods Inwards	Delivery Note	Insp	
XII.	Hardware & Software Integration		Hardware & Software Integration Procedure				
XIII.	Hardware & Developed Software Acceptance	Verification	Quality manual	Programmer	Check List & Acceptance Specification	DA	Wit
XIV.	Create User & Maintenance Manuals	Design/ Project Control	Standard Format for User Manuals	Programmer	Standard format	DA	
XV.	Dismantle for Shipment		Quality Manual	Tech Services	Check List	Insp.	
XVI.	Project Review 3	Design/ Project Verification	Project Review Minutes Check List	Project Manager	Project Review Minutes		
XVII	Site Survey		Quality Manual Site Survey Procedure	Project Manager	Check List	Visit	
XVII	Installation & Commissioning	Verification	Quality manual Installation & Commissioning Procedures	Project Manager	Acceptance Specification	Insp.	Wit

Quality in Project Management

XIX.	Customer Acceptance/ Handover		Handover Certification	Project Manager	Hand-over Certificate	Insp(full)	Wit
XX.	Software & Document-ation Archiving	Records	Archiving	Project Manager	Various		
XXI.	Final Report	Records	Project Control	Project Manger	Project Summary	DA	

Table 5.2 Quality Plan for a Software Project

Description of Checks used in Table 5.2		
Key	Explanation	Approved or checked by
Cust.	Customer	
DR100%	100% Examination of documentation for Review & Approval	Peer
DR(sample)	Sample Examination of the documentation for approval	Peer
DA(ind)	Independent approval of document	Project Mgr. & Peer
DA	Approval of document	Peer
Insp	Inspection activity	Peer
Insp(Full)	Full Inspection & Test of System	Project Mgr.
Org.	Organisation	
Visit	Visit Customer & Inspection	Project Mgr.
Wit	Witnessed by customer	Project Mgr. & Customer

Table 5.3 Descriptions of Checks

Quality in Project Management

Quality Control

Quality Control means looking at specific project results to see if they comply with the standards set and the Quality Plan identifies when this will be done. Again this is not just the product results but also the project process results. Examples of process results that may be measured are the costs of the project versus budget.

The elements for project control have already been considered earlier, but they are also the key to quality in project management. A checklist that has been developed and used successfully on a number of projects is given below. However, like all check lists it is not exhaustive and should be used as a guide.

- Customer requirements should be understood and agreed, including specification assurance, document control, document validation and verification methods and project sizing.
- Communication routes with the customer should be defined and the project structure and hierarchy detailed.
- Risk Management & Risk Assessment Techniques should be applied at an early stage in the project.
- Project and Quality Plans need to be regularly up dated and reviewed. Reviews, monitoring and inspection methods should be established, including; Cost, Specification, Time and Health & Safety.
- Project Quality Responsibilities should be clear. The Project Manager or Leader responsibilities need to be agreed. Usually those are to meet the project specification and deliver the project on time and to budget. Try asking a few project managers, what they believe their responsibilities are, you will receive some very strange answers!
- Team Building and awareness of the project objectives, aims and goals.
- Codes of Practice and Procedures need to be easily understood and not be over burdening. These may be based on ISO 9001.
- Project Records need to be readily available and maintained. Configuration management procedures associated with the management of change need to be established and operated.
- Suppliers (Supplier Quality Control) or Raw Material Control (both for any equipment trials and on going) need to be evaluated and chosen.

Quality in Project Management

- Deliverables: Validation - the means of establishing that the deliverables have been satisfactorily completed and handed over to the customer, i.e. the project inputs equate to the project outputs. This can be achieved through a number of methods; final review or inspection and test of the contract or terms of reference for the project against the deliverables sent to the customer.
- Project Audit - are they necessary on a project of this size? What should be the scope and frequency of the audits?
- Corrective and Preventive Action - has the means been establish to log, action, monitor and close customer feedback and supplier problems.
- Problem Resolution can be achieved through the use of a number of different techniques such as; Force Field Analysis, Cause & Effect Analysis, etc.
- Project Closure - see deliverables plus archiving and closing the project internally. Including formal feedback from the customer regarding (quality) performance and a project lessons learnt review.
- Post project review - lessons learnt

The outputs from the operation of quality control will be actions to improve the operation of the project. There may also be improvements that can be used in future projects that should be handed to the organisation for consideration. Non-conformances identified should be dealt with according to non-conformance procedures and change controls.

Quality Assurance

[handwritten: Serraus of activities to achieve QA - preventia]

This is really the quality control of the quality planning. It is all those planned and systematic actions necessary to provide adequate confidence that a product or service will satisfy given requirements for quality.

A Quality Assurance Management System (QAMS) standard is a model that management can employ to give guidance to the selection of appropriate quality assurance controls. It is possible to apply a QAMS to most key areas and processes and in most stages of supply of the product or service and the project management process is no different.

What is a QAMS?

In order to regulate a process, (whether the process is an aircraft control system, a manufacturing sequence or a design and development process), it is necessary to have some formal method of control and feedback, otherwise the system may become unstable or go out of control.

Quality in Project Management

Figure 5.2 A Control System

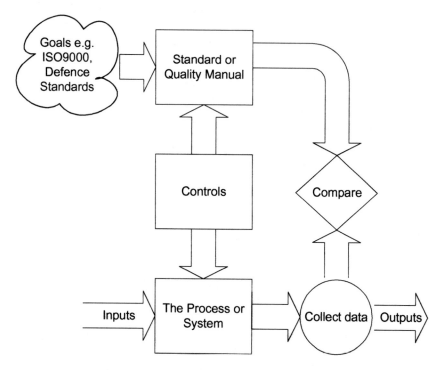

A simple control system is described in Figure 5.2. There is an *input* to the system (possibly data or raw materials). The *process* then manipulates the data or material, providing an *output* in terms of an acceptable or unacceptable finished product (the process deliverable). If the process consists of data manipulation, the output could be a report - controls are necessary to avoid the production of an inaccurate report.

There will be a *goal* that could be costs, quantity, delivery targets or the QAMS model - ISO 9000. This goal will need interpretation into a *Standard* or possibly the *Quality Manual*.

There will be a feedback mechanism to control the process allowing timely action to be taken to avoid failure to achieve the goal. This could involve *collection of data* regarding the performance of the process and a *comparison* with the goal, possibly by performing an audit. If the comparison indicates an unacceptable trend, *controls* as described in the Quality System or Quality Manual may need to be updated or improved.

Quality in Project Management

Quality Management Tools

There are tools and techniques available to assist in managing quality within the project as well as some that help to maintain quality in planning the project.

Inspections, including reviews

Reviews are considered in detail in the Project Review section. Inspection would include measuring, examining and testing to see if results meet the requirements.

Control charts

These are graphical displays of results over time of the process. They are used to see if a process is 'in control'. They may be used to monitor output variables e.g. cost vs budget.

Pareto Analysis

Establishing the factors that together make up all the various causes of overruns in projects invariably means that a considerable number of problems are discovered. To tackle all these problems at one go would require enormous resources and in many cases some of the problems may be trivial and not worth pursuing for the time being.

A technique invaluable in singling out those problems that have the greatest influence on the project is Pareto Analysis.

Very often when this type of analysis is conducted, the results show that when placed in order of importance out of a given number of causes, only a small percentage, usually around 20%, account for 80% of the total problems. For this reason the concept is often known as the 80 - 20 rule.

Guidelines for Pareto Analysis:

- Select the factor to be analysed. Determine how the data is to be collected and what the duration of data collection will be.
- Rank the data in ascending order.
- Establish the appropriate horizontal scale and vertical scale.

Quality in Project Management

The object of Pareto Analysis is to identify 'THE IMPORTANT FEW' with a view to avoiding 'THE TRIVIAL MANY'. Thus, it is possible to make an 80% improvement by tackling and eliminating only 20% of the problems.

Cause and Effect Diagrams

This is a technique often used in quality management to identify how various causes and sub-causes relate to potential problems. It can be very a useful tool for the project team.

These diagrams provide a means of logically analysing a problem with a view to tackling the root cause. Generally the construction of a Cause and Effect Diagram is a team exercise. The diagram is to formalise and to keep a record of the team's logical approach to the problem. This provides a method by which the team's thoughts and deliberations can be documented, and provides a catalyst for discussing the problem.

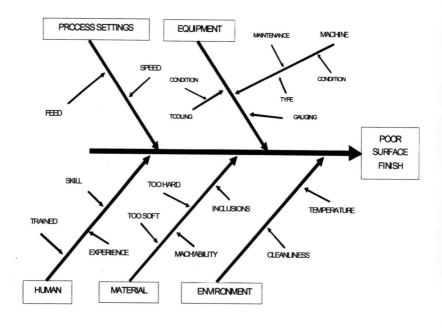

Figure 5.4 Cause & Effect Diagram

Quality in Project Management

Cause and Effect Guidelines

The first stage is to clearly define the problem. This definition may be provided from a Pareto Analysis or from statistical process control data. The diagram records from a fixed point what the team considers are the main causes of the problem, such as human, material, machines, environment, sequence, procedure, process system, equipment etc. Having determined the major group causes, the team brainstorms the likely sub-causes within the major groups and possibly the further sub-causes.

Having established the team's views on possible suspects or causes of the problem, the team next needs to consider which, in their view, is the most likely culprit. The possible causes can be ranked in order of most likely, most easy to eliminate from the investigations etc.

Having prioritised the most probable culprits an action plan for investigation can be drawn up and implemented. This plan would detail the most likely causes, the method of evaluation and who is responsible for conducting the investigation. This stage would be repeated until the actual guilty party was discovered.

Bench marking/ Measuring Quality Performance

This is comparing actual or planned project practices to those of other projects to identify areas for improvement. They could be compared against other internal projects or, via industry standards, against other organisations. It is based on the same process as that for measuring quality performance for any business process or product, since managing a project is just another business process.

All organisations need to establish and quantify the key factors with which to monitor their quality performance. It is not enough to believe that the organisation's quality performance has always been satisfactory. Agreement needs to be reached as to what the key factors are by which to judge the quality performance. What is the organisation's current performance against these factors and how can the current quality performance be improved? If measures of quality performance are not established and monitored then adverse and possibly catastrophic trends may not be identified with possible dire consequences for the organisation concerned. Juran talks about breakthrough and control to new levels of quality performance. Organisations that can achieve this objective will always be successful because they will be continually improving.

Quality in Project Management

Quality performance measures need to be established, not only at a corporate level but at all levels throughout the organisation, even down to an individual unit or person. Quality Performance measurement is one of the most important ways of improving the quality performance of organisations. If the current quality performance is not known then improvements can only be subjective and not quantifiable.

Having established and measured an organisation's, department's or project's performance indicators, these values need to be compared - bench marked - against recognised leaders or pacesetters. This is to determine if the current performance is of the correct standard - *World Class*.

Quality in Project Management

Guidelines for Bench Marking:

Firstly, senior management need to agree the necessity for establishing quality performance and then this must be communicated to all levels throughout the organisation to gain commitment and understanding. Departmental Purpose Analysis and Customer/Supplier investigations can be used to help convince personnel of the need for quality performance measurement. The project team need to agree the Performance Measures.

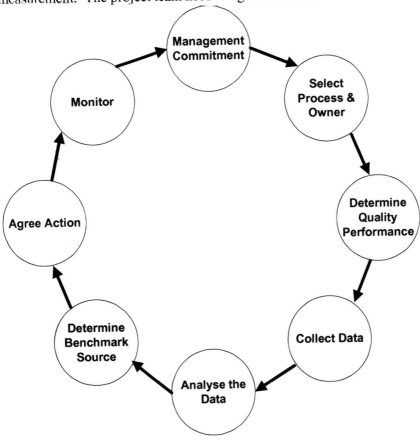

Figure 5.3 Benchmarking sequence

Next, the actual project processes that need to be monitored have to be established and agreed. Having established the processes to be monitored then the factors critical to success need to be determined.

Quality in Project Management

These critical success factors or quality performance measurements should be:

- Suitable for the particular process, department or organisation evaluated – in this case the project process.
- Consistent, so that there is no doubt about the method of calculation of the performance measure and therefore data for performance measurement can be accurately and reliably obtained.
- Clear, and residing with a particular project team so that responsibility or ownership for achieving the performance criteria is understood.
- Easily and regularly calculated, usually numbering between 3 and 7 performance measures.
- Clearly defined start and finish.
- Defined direction not a solution.
- Achievable and within the groups' capability.
- Possibly determined from the customer/supplier relationship and the department purpose analysis.

The performance measurement categories can be broken down into two main categories, quantifiable "Hard Standards" and non-quantifiable (subjective) "Soft Standards".

"Hard Standards" are measurable such that an agreed performance target can be set. Examples of such standards could be:

- Cost - Costs/item, transactions/employee
- Quality - Number of overruns, complaints
- Service - Time to response to stakeholder queries; time to update the plan.

"Soft Standards", although not always directly measurable these standards are as equally important as hard standards. These soft standards can make the difference between an existing customer returning, obtaining a new customer or placating a dissatisfied customer.

Soft Standards can include:
- Personnel style - Friendly, helpful, positive approach
- Efficient service - Anticipate needs, be flexible, provide clear information, professionalism
- Concern - Manage problems - when troubles do occur understanding the customer's difficulties and helping resolve the problem.

Quality in Project Management

Data collection:
Having determined the quality performance standards that need to be monitored the next stage would be to agree how to quantify the current performance level and start to collect the data on a regular basis. The data collected could include:

- Customer satisfaction; this could be quantified by surveys of both existing and potential customers. Analysis of service and project performance.
- Process efficiency; by monitoring cost overruns, number of revisions. Analysis of processes to determine wasted time, labour and process utilisation, examination of the number of changes.
- Environmental losses, waste of resources, human and energy, could be quantified and monitored by employee surveys, interviews (e.g. exit or leaving interviews) and energy audits.

Analysis:
With the current performance level determined the project team or departmental personnel would need to agree new targets. These new targets can either be agreed with the customer (internal or external), or alternatively, the targets may be based on other recognised leaders or pacesetters - the organisations who are seen as being World Class or best in class. This information can be obtained from: surveys (customer and competition), technical journals, review of advertisements etc.

Obtaining the Bench Mark Source: There are a number of possible benchmark sources.

Internal Bench Marking against a similar national or international division. This is the easiest as access to the required information should be relatively straightforward.

Industrial Bench Marking against the competition. This is obviously more difficult as competitors are unlikely to be keen on releasing commercially sensitive information. However, Trade Associations can be helpful and information scientists can provide useful information. There are also best practice clubs now available that share approaches and information.

Quality in Project Management

Action Plan & Monitoring:
Having obtained what is seen as being a suitable target then work can commence towards establishing an action plan for improving the performance to meet the new performance criteria.

BS ISO 10006: 1997

Guidelines to Quality in Project Management

The standard provides guidance on how quality management systems can assist in achieving a quality project. It will also help project managers ensure that ISO9000 standards are followed by a project. Quality in projects does not just mean the quality of the deliverable – which is of course important, but also the quality of the process used – this can have wider implications throughout the organisation.

Many of these processes have already been considered earlier in the book and Table 5.7 allows you to reference these processes within the text. In addition you are recommended to read a copy of this standard to appreciate its role in project management.

Contents of ISO10006: 1997

Section	ISO section	Book Section
1	Scope	-
2	Normative references	-
3	Definitions	Project Definition
4	Project characteristics	Project Definition
4.1	General	Project Definition, Project Environment
4.2	Project Management	Project Definition
4.3	Organisation	Projects and Company Organisation Structure
4.4	Project Phases and project processes	Project Life Cycle
5	Quality in project management processes	Project Quality Management Processes
5.1	General	-

Quality in Project Management

5.2	Strategic process	Control and Review of Projects
5.3	Interdependency management processes	Initiation, planning, change and configuration – Project Planning Process
5.4	Scope-related processes	Project Planning
5.5.	Time-related processes	Time Schedule
5.6	Cost-related processes	Budget
5.7	Resource-related processes	Budget
5.8	Personnel-related processes	People
5.9	Communication-related processes	Control and Review of Projects
5.10	Risk-related processes	Risk Assessment
5.11	Purchasing-related processes	Budget
6	Learning from the project	Project Final Report

Table 5.4 Correlation of ISO sections with the Sections in this book

BS 6079:2000

This standard is a "Guide to Project Management". It provides guidance to the following people:

- General managers – to raise awareness of project management issues
- Project managers – to improve their ability to manage projects
- Project support staff – to help understand the project environment
- Educators and trainers – to understand the industrial context that a project will have to operate in

Its aim is to highlight the sort of management problems that can be encountered in a project environment and to provide some possible solutions.

The contents of this standard, has to a large extent, been covered elsewhere in the text. However, a brief overview is given of each section and Table 5.8 indicates where to find further details. In addition you are recommended to read a copy of this standard to appreciate its role in project management.

Quality in Project Management

Section	BS Title	Book Section
1	General	-
1.1	Scope	-
1.2	References	-
1.3	Definitions	Project Definitions
2	The Corporate Aspects of Project Management	Projects and Company Organisation Structure
2.1	General	-
2.2	Nature of projects	Project Definition
2.3	The work to be done	Work Breakdown Structure
2.4	The project life cycle	Project Life Cycle
2.5	The benefits of project management	Planning Concepts
3	Project and Organisational structures	Projects and Company Organisation Structure
3.1	General	-
3.2	The hierarchical functional organisation	Projects and Company Organisation Structure
3.3	The matrix organisation	Projects and Company Organisation Structure
3.4	The project organisation	Projects and Company Organisation Structure
3.5	Criteria for reorganisation	Projects and Company Organisation Structure
4	The project management process	Managing the planning process
4.1	General	-
4.2	The project management process – introduction	Phases in the Project Life Cycle
4.3	The project management process – planning	Phases in the Project Life Cycle
4.4	The project management process – control	Control and Review of Projects
4.5	The project plan	Managing the planning process
4.6	Processes supporting the project management process	Managing the planning process

Quality in Project Management

4.7	Project personnel development	People
5	Project Lifecycle	Project Life Cycle
5.1	General	-
5.2	Types of project	-
5.3	Project phasing	Phases in the Project Life Cycle
5.4	Project phase sequence	Phases in the Project Life Cycle
5.5	Description of phase content	Phases in the Project Life Cycle

Table 5.5 Correlation of ISO sections with the Sections in this book

Section 1 is an introduction and overview. Section 2 is aimed at senior management and covers the nature of projects, the need for clear planning and control, management of project staff and the benefits of project management. The project life cycle is considered and the importance of feasibility studies and planning. At an early stage senior management would normally establish a reporting structure and some key milestones with deliverables that would be used to release the next phases of funding. Section 3 is aimed at operational managers and discusses the effect that the structure of an organisation can have on the project operation. The organisational structures considered are functional, matrix and project. As well as discussing the pros and cons of these different organisational structures, the politics and psychological of organisational change is considered. Section 4 is also aimed at operational managers and looks at the project management process. The standard describes a generic project management process and the guidance provided can be applied to projects of any size and any industrial sector. Guidance is provided on planning (including establishing project organisation, authorities, incentives, communication, work breakdown structures and statement of work) and control (including controlling the project plan, budgets, progressing the project).

Quality in Project Management

This section also considers some of the processes that support project management: quality assurance, configuration management, risk management, procurement, financial management and personnel development.

The final section looks at the project lifecycle and considers the phases within the project. The five fundamental project phases are conception, feasibility, implementation, operation and termination.

Index

Index

Index

Accent, 19
Activity Listings, 156
Activity on Arrow, 148, 150
Activity on Node, 147
Audits, 129
Balanced Matrix, 100
Bar Charts, 60
Benchmarking, 181
Brainstorming, 77, 78, 79, 80
Budget, 124, 135, 139, 143, 167, 185
Cause and Effect Diagrams, 178
Change Control, 116, 117
Change Environment, 92
Communication Process, 10, 11
Conception, 102, 104
Constraints, 136, 139
Cost, 106, 114, 118, 124, 125, 141, 174, 182, 185
Crash, 119, 159
Critical Path Analysis, 139, 152
Cultural Influences, 95
Desk Research, 49
Diagrams, 40, 178
Diction, 19
Discretionary dependencies, 146
Discussion, 78, 79, 82, 83, 85
Documentation, 114, 173
Duration, 153, 154, 159
Earned value, 124
Earned Value, 124
Exception Report, 126
Experimentation, 49
Expert Judgement, 155
External dependencies, 146
Extranet, 115
Feasibility, 102, 105
Film, 76
Financial Report, 126
Flip charts, 75

Fog Index, 29
Framework, 66
Fully blocked layout, 36
Functional Language, 26
Functional Organisation, 96
GANTT, 110, 135, 157, 158
Goals, 118, 136
Grade, 164
Graphs, 42, 63
Hard Standards, 182
Headings, 71
Highlight Report, 126
Highlighting, 71
Histogram, 62
House style, 38
Images, 39
Imaginative Language, 27
Implementation, 102, 108
Interview, 18, 50
ISO 10006, 184
ISO 9001, 174
Lags, 146
Leads, 146
Life Cycle, 5, 102, 103, 104, 184, 186, 187
Listening, 14, 46, 49
Literature Surveys, 54
Magnetic boards, 76
Mandatory dependencies, 146
Materials, 118, 140, 167
Matrix Organisation, 99
Meetings, 80, 81, 82, 122
Memoranda, 34
Milestone, 157
Network, 110, 113, 145, 146, 149, 150, 151
Note taking, 57, 59
Numbering, 71
Operation, 102
Operational Work, 90

Index

Oral Communication, 17, 18
Organisational Culture, 94
Outdated expressions, 28
Pareto Analysis, 177, 178, 179
Passive Writing, 30
Personal Language, 27
PERT, 139, 152, 153, 158
Photographs, 40
Pictogram, 62
Pie Charts, 64
Plan, 106, 123, 134, 135, 137, 145, 166, 167, 168, 170, 173, 174, 184
Planning, 73, 84, 102, 103, 107, 133, 136, 145, 158, 165, 166, 167, 185, 186
Power Verbs, 30
Precedence, 146, 148
Preventive Action, 127, 175
Programme Management, 92
Project Management, 1, 5, 6, 52, 87, 89, 91, 161, 163, 184, 185, 186
Project Organisation, 98
Project Plan, 131, 134, 170, 185
Project Review, 120, 122, 123, 129, 171, 172, 177
Project Work, 90, 135
Proposal, 45, 102, 104
Quality, 5, 52, 53, 54, 55, 90, 93, 114, 119, 121, 123, 135, 161, 163, 164, 165, 166, 167, 168, 170, 172, 173, 174, 175, 176, 177, 179, 180, 182, 184
Quality Assurance, 5, 55, 121, 163, 165, 166, 167, 175

Quality Control, 165, 167, 168, 174
Quality Environment, 93
Quality Planning, 165, 166, 167
Questionnaire, 50, 51
Reactive Control, 118
Real Objects, 77
Regulations, 94
Report, 38, 45, 65, 70, 71, 124, 126, 127, 173, 185
Resources, 118
Risk, 135, 137, 138, 174, 185
Sampling, 51
Scope, 102, 118, 184, 185, 186
SMART, 105
Soft Standards, 182
Speed, 19
Spider Diagram, 59
Stakeholders, 92
Standards, 89, 91, 94, 182
Status Report, 124
Strategic Environment, 92
Style, 27, 70, 79
Tables, 42, 63
Task, 111, 112, 127, 148
Telephone, 20, 50, 170
Termination, 102, 109
Time, 80, 105, 118, 153, 154, 167, 174, 182, 185
Tone, 20, 33
Video, 18, 42, 76
Visual Aids, 42, 75
Vocal Qualities, 19
Whiteboards, 75
Work Breakdown, 5, 110, 134, 135, 139, 186
Written Communication, 22